PROGRAMMING IN

C++

Stephen C. Dewhurst • Kathy T. Stark

AT&T Bell Laboratories
Summit, New Jersey

 Prentice Hall, Englewood Cliffs, New Jersey 07632

Library of Congress Cataloging-in-Publication Data

Dewhurst, Stephen C.
     Programming in C++.
     (Prentice Hall software series)
     Bibliography: p.
     Includes index.
     1. C++ (Computer program language) I. Stark,
Kathy T. II. Title. III. Title: Programming in C
plus plus. IV. Series: Prentice-Hall software series.
QA76.73.C153D49 1989   005.13'3   89-8391
ISBN 013723156-3

Editorial/production supervision: Karen Skrable Fortgang
Cover design: Lundgren Graphics, Ltd.
Manufacturing buyer: Robert Anderson

UNIX® is a registered trademark of AT&T.

Prentice Hall Software Series, Brian W. Kernighan, *Advisor*

The publisher offers discounts on this book when ordered in bulk
quantities. For more information write:
   Special Sales/College Marketing
   Prentice-Hall, Inc.
   College Technical and Reference Division
   Englewood Cliffs, NJ 07632

Printed in the United States of America

10 9 8 7 6 5 4

ISBN 0-13-723156-3

Prentice-Hall International (UK) Limited, *London*
Prentice-Hall of Australia Pty. Limited, *Sydney*
Prentice-Hall Canada Inc., *Toronto*
Prentice-Hall Hispanoamericana, S.A., *Mexico*
Prentice-Hall of India Private Limited, *New Delhi*
Prentice-Hall of Japan, Inc., *Tokyo*
Simon & Schuster Asia Pte. Ltd., *Singapore*
Editora Prentice-Hall do Brasil, Ltda., *Rio de Janeiro*

Contents

Preface

C++ has become an increasingly popular programming language. Its appeal is due not only to the popularity of its parent language C, but also to its data abstraction and object-oriented features. The development of C++ has been marked by an active dialog among a community of users who contributed to the language's formation with a fertile exchange of ideas. The result is that C++ is a language with a rich range of features that supports a variety of programming methods and techniques.

The C++ language can best be understood by observing how the language features work together in writing programs. As both users and implementors of C++ at a time when the language was being formed, we had the unusual opportunity to see why certain language features were developed and to participate in their refinement through implementation and use. In this book, we hope to share our understanding and appreciation of C++ as a programming tool.

We wrote this book at a time when C++ was still evolving. Our presentation of C++ tries to avoid details that might cause confusion among users of different versions of the language, however, new features like multiple inheritance and refinements to the language definition and implementation might make the language we present somewhat different from the implementation the reader has available. We did not intend to write a language reference manual or a description of a particular implementation. We did intend to guide our readers beyond the details of the features to general concepts of program design that help programmers use C++ effectively.

This book has benefited by contributions made by many of those who participated in the development of C++. We gratefully acknowledge the contributions made by many individuals to the development of C++ programming methodologies and techniques. Their thoughts have influenced us greatly, and many of their ideas have found their way into this book: Tom Cargill, Jim Coplien, Keith Gorlen, Bill Hopkins, Andy Koenig, Jerry Schwarz, and Jon Shopiro are chief among these pioneers. We would also like to thank our colleagues Laura Eaves, Phil Brown, and Stan Lippman, who worked with us in the development of a C++ compiler; Sarah Hewins, Bob Wilson, and Wayne Wolf, who reviewed various drafts of the manuscript; and Jeff Monin, who lent us his time and expertise at several key points. John Wait of Prentice-Hall provided motivation and guidance for this project from start to finish.

To Brian Kernighan our debt is of an entirely different order. Brian persevered through many versions of the manuscript, guiding us from obscurity towards clarity. That we may not have completed the journey reflects more on our stubbornness than his perseverance and persuasion.

Bjarne Stroustrup not only originated C++ and evolved it into a rich programming language, but he was willing to argue about it on the way. We thank Bjarne for many valuable discussions and disputations, as well as for his support for this project.

S.C.D.

K.T.S.

CHAPTER 0: **Introduction**

C++ is a general purpose programming language derived from C. It adds to its parent language a number of features, the most important of which are those supporting data abstraction and object-oriented programming. C++ retains most of its C heritage, and has adopted C's basic data types, operations, statement syntax, and program structure. Added features enhance the C-like parts of the language as well as support new programming techniques.

Programming languages are not produced by spontaneous generation, but are in effect generated by shifts in the way people think about the process of programming. Generalized and codified, these thought processes achieve the status of paradigms, and new languages are created to support them. Programming paradigms, then, are models that provide sets of techniques to be applied when designing and implementing programs. These techniques address issues such as how a design relates to a programming problem, the use of abstraction, and program organization. A language supports a particular paradigm if the features of that language make it easy to apply the techniques of that model. The features of C++ support a range of programming paradigms.

Most books on new programming languages teach the language features but abandon the reader to discover alone the process of programming in the language. For a language like C++, which is significantly richer than most languages with which the reader may be familiar, this approach is unsatisfactory. This book is about how to *program* using C++. We discuss the details of how to use C++ features, as well as how to apply paradigms in design and implementation.

Our presentation progressively develops concepts in order to place both programming paradigms and language features in context. Although we cover most features, we do not present a minutely detailed description of the language. Many of our examples make use of UNIX operating system functions without detailed explanation, but their use is straightforward

1

enough that it should not impede understanding for a reader unfamiliar with the UNIX system. We assume our readers are experienced programmers familiar with C, and we go into the most detail in presenting what the C programmer finds new when programming in C++.

0.1 The C++ Language

The major addition C++ makes to C is the introduction of class types. Classes allow a user to define aggregate data types that include not only data members but also functions that operate on the type. Data hiding in classes provides the mechanism for data abstraction. Class inheritance extends data abstraction to object-oriented programming. User-defined operator functions and conversions enable classes to be integrated into the predefined type system, by allowing class type operands in expressions and conversions among class and nonclass types.

Classes include features that enable memory management to be built into dynamic data structures. The language also provides general dynamic allocation and deallocation operators. This combination allows a programmer to tailor a memory management scheme to a specific application.

Besides the features that support techniques for building data structures, there are also those that enhance the use of functions. All C++ function declarations must include argument type information. This allows argument type checking and function overloading. Function argument declarations may also include default values for arguments not given in a function call. Reference types in C++ allow arguments to be passed by reference, as well as by value.

0.2 Programming Paradigms

Programming paradigms are models of how to design and implement programs. Different models result in different techniques. That the techniques are different does not imply they are in conflict, and various techniques can be seen to complement one another. What programming models seem to have in common are the notions that the design should be based on abstractions that correspond to elements in the programming problem, and that the implementation should be a collection of modules, preferably reusable ones. They differ on how to form the abstractions and what constitutes a module.

The well-established methods of procedural programming are based on a model of building a program as a collection of functions. The techniques provide guidance on how to design, organize, and implement the functions that make up a program. The design method of functional decomposition identifies the functions that serve as the abstract operations that solve a programming problem. File organization allows functions to be grouped in separate modules, and structured programming techniques make the implementation of a function readable and maintainable.

Data abstraction focuses on the data structures that are neglected by procedure-oriented techniques. The model of data abstraction is that a data structure should be defined by the operations on it, rather than the structure of its implementation. The technique used for data abstraction is to encapsulate a data structure in an abstract data type. Access to the structure is provided through a set of operations that are part of the type. Data abstraction complements the procedural programming view of functions as abstract operations because neither abstraction is complete without the other.

Object-oriented programming is based on a model of building programs as a collection of abstract data type instances. Object-oriented design identifies the types that represent objects in the programming problem. The operations in the object types are, like the functions in the procedural programming model, the abstract operations that solve the problem. The object type serves as a module that can be reused for solving another problem in the same domain.

No single paradigm is suitable for solving all programming problems well. Programming requires engineering expertise but is not yet a science. Programming techniques need to be applied flexibly, with an eye to how well they suit the problem at hand. Blind application of the currently most popular paradigm is never a substitute for careful examination and thoughtful abstraction of a problem. A major goal of this book is to encourage the reader to think, both critically and flexibly, about problems in program design and implementation.

0.3 Book Organization

We intend to teach the reader how to design and implement programs using C++. This book's organization interweaves presentation of the C++ language with discussion of the techniques and paradigms for which the features were designed. We start with the data types and operations of the language, proceed through ways of organizing data structures and operations into programs, and end with the advanced topics of memory management and library design.

One view of programs is that they describe a sequence of operations on data, and so the C++ data types and operations are presented in Chapter 1. The language features adopted from C can be seen to provide abstract data types and operations, such as numbers and arithmetic operations. User-defined class types are presented as a means of adding both data types and operations to the language.

Chapter 2 discusses procedural programming techniques for organizing sequences of operations into functions. Functional decomposition and structured programming are covered as design paradigms, along with supporting language features of scope and linkage of names, parameter passing by value and reference, overloading of function names, default arguments, and inline functions.

Chapter 3 covers the basic features of C++ classes. This straightforward presentation of language features provides the underpinnings on which much of the rest of the book is based. We cover data and function members, constructors and destructors, operator overloading, and protection.

Chapter 4 discusses the use of classes for data abstraction. We show how to develop a new data type, using the facilities provided by classes to make the implementation secure and maintainable, and how to define conversions and operations that integrate the new type into the existing type system.

Chapter 5 covers class inheritance, a feature that allows a new class type to be defined in terms of existing class types. Inheritance can be used to modify an existing abstract data type, create hierarchical collections of related abstract types, combine the properties of unrelated types, and provide flexible runtime binding of function calls.

Chapter 6 applies the use of data abstraction and inheritance to object-oriented programming design. We present guidelines for designing and organizing a program as object type modules and demonstrate the dynamic object-oriented programming style.

Chapter 7 presents the memory management features of C++. Efficient and maintainable memory management schemes can be developed and tailored for general use, for a given library or class type, or for a specific application.

In Chapter 8 we discuss the design and use of libraries as collections of reusable software modules. We show how to design libraries so that they are extensible and modifiable by their users without affecting the library source code.

The last section of each chapter contains exercises. Those marked with a † have solutions given in the Appendix.

We relate the details of the C++ language to larger problems of software design and engineering. We hope our readers learn not only how to use C++ effectively as a programming tool, but are also stimulated to think in new ways about the process of designing and implementing programs.

CHAPTER 1: **Data Types and Operations**

The C++ type system consists of basic language-defined types, user-defined class types, and types that can be derived from the basic and class types. The language provides operations and standard conversions for the built-in types. Class types can also have operations and conversions defined for them, thus allowing classes to be used as consistent extensions of the predefined type system.

The built-in data types in C++ can be interpreted as abstract concepts, such as numbers or boolean values, or according to their representation in the computer as a sequence of bits. The interpretation depends on the operations used to manipulate the values of the different types. The arithmetic and logical operators give results that preserve the mathematical and logical interpretations of the types. Other operators give results that depend on and reveal the bit representation.

1.1 Numeric Types

C++ has both integer and floating point numeric types. The language provides arithmetic operators that are overloaded to work with both integer and floating point values, and defines conversions among the numeric types. Overloaded operators are those operators for which the same symbol represents more than one distinct implementation of an operation. The numeric types, when used with arithmetic operators, are interpreted as representations of numbers.

The following program does a calculation using numeric variables and values with arithmetic operators. To represent integers `int` values are used, and `double` floating point values are used to represent real numbers.

```
#include <stdio.h>

main() {
/*
    Distance of a falling object from the point of its
    release at each of the first 10 seconds of its fall,
    in meters
*/
    const double g = 9.80;  // acceleration from gravity

    for( int t = 1; t <= 10; t++ ) {
        double distance =  g * t * t / 2;
        printf( "\t%2d %7.2f\n", t, distance );
    }
}
```

The program prints out the distance an object has fallen at each of the first ten seconds after being dropped:

```
 1 ·   4.90
 2    19.60
 3    44.10
 4    78.40
 5   122.50
 6   176.40
 7   240.10
 8   313.60
 9   396.90
10   490.00
```

The expression calculating the distance mixes `double` and `int` type operands. The result is a `double` value that is stored in the `double` variable `distance`.

```
    double distance =  g * t * t / 2;
```

Although both `t` and `2` have type `int`, the calculation is done completely with floating point operations. Because `g` has type `double`, and the multiplications and division group left to right, each operator in the calculation has at least one `double` operand that forces the conversion of the `int` operand to match it.

The arithmetic operators are overloaded for the numeric types. The types of the operands determine whether an integer or floating point operation is done. If the expression is changed so that the operations are done in a different order, the types of some of the operations may also change.

```
distance = g * ( t * t / 2 );
```

With parentheses forcing the grouping of the integer operands, there is an integer multiplication of t by t producing an int result. The division is also applied to int operands. The integer division has an int type result; when t is odd the fractional part of the result is lost, and this calculation produces different results from the previous one with floating point operations. Using a floating point literal for the divisor forces the operation to be floating point division, and the result returns to the previous accuracy.

```
distance = g * ( t * t / 2.0 );
```

For an overloaded operator, the types of the operands affect which implementation of the operator is used to perform the operation.

The arithmetic operators are defined to work for operands of several numeric types. The unary operators are increment ++, decrement --, negation -, and no-op +. The binary arithmetic operators are multiplication *, division /, addition +, and subtraction -. In addition, the remainder operator % works only on integer operands.

The increment and decrement operators have the side effect of changing the value of the object that is their operand. They can be used in either prefix or postfix form with different results. In the prefix form, the result of the expression is that of the object after it was incremented or decremented. In the postfix form, the expression value is that of the object before it is changed. Other arithmetic operators do not change the value of their operands.

Unary operators have higher precedence than binary operators. The multiplicative binary operators *, /, and % have higher precedence than the additive operators + and -.

The integer types are char, short, int, and long. Each type can represent at least the range of values as the previous type on the list, so each can be thought of as larger or equal in size to the preceding type. The integer types come in both signed and unsigned versions. In declarations, short, int, and long type specifiers mean the signed versions of these types unless unsigned is explicitly specified. When different types of integer operands are combined in an expression, they are converted to be the same type. Operands of type char and short are always converted at least to int. Other conversions are always to the larger of the operand types. Conversions are only made to the unsigned version of a type if one operand type is unsigned and larger or equal in size to the other operand type.

The floating point types are `float`, `double`, and `long double`. Each type can represent at least the set of values of the previous type on the list, so each can be thought of as containing the preceding type. When different floating point types are combined as operands in an arithmetic expression, the smaller-sized operand is converted to the same type as the other operand. When floating point and integer operands are combined, the integer is converted to the same type as the floating point operand.

Any numeric value can be assigned to an object of any other numeric type, in which case the value is converted to the type on the left-hand side of the assignment.

```
double d;
d = 42;
```

The conversion may result in loss of part of the value.

```
int i;
i = 3.1415;
char c;
c = 777;
```

In the above, `i` is given the value 3. The value 777 is probably too large to be represented in a `char`, so the value of `c` after the assignment depends on how a particular implementation does the conversion from the larger- to smaller-sized integer type.

Conversion operators, or *casts*, can be used for explicit conversions. For example, in the following, the `int` value of `count` is explicitly converted to `double`.

```
int count = 1066, total = 1337;
double ratio;

ratio = double( count ) / total;
```

This example uses a function-call style cast:

```
double( count )
```

An alternative form of the same cast operation is:

```
( double )count
```

The function-call form is usually considered the clearer style in simple conversion expressions.

Numeric values can be directly represented in a program as numeric literals. Floating point literals may have a decimal point and a fractional part, and also an exponent:

```
9.80
0.98e1
98e-1
```

These literals all represent the same value and have type `double`. For values of different floating point types, the suffix `L` or `l` indicates `long double`, and `F` or `f` indicates `float`.

```
0.98e1L
9.80f
```

Integer literals have type `int` unless their value is too large or their type is indicated with a suffix. A literal value too large to be represented as an `int` may have type `long`. A suffix `L` or `l` indicates a `long`, and `U` or `u` indicates `unsigned`. These suffixes may be combined, for example:

```
1642UL
```

An octal literal is indicated with a 0 first digit:

```
0777
```

A hexadecimal literal is indicated with a leading `0x` or `0X`:

```
0x1ff
```

Numeric values may also be represented symbolically by using a `const` with an initializing value.

```
const double g = 9.80;
```

Because the `const` indicates that the value of `g` cannot be changed, the identifier always represents its value `9.80`.

Integer values may also be represented symbolically by members of `enum` lists. If not otherwise initialized, the `enum` members have successive `int` values, with the first one having the value 0.

```
enum { mon, tues, wed, thur, fri, sat, sun };
```

Here, `fri` has the value 4. When `enum` members are explicitly initialized, uninitialized members of the list have values that are one more than the previous value on the list.

```
enum { mon = 1, tues, wed, thur, fri, sat = -1, sun };
```

In this case, the value of `fri` is 5, and the value of `sun` is 0.

The character set is represented by integer values that can be contained in a `char` data type. Character literals, which are characters or escape sequences in single quotes, provide a convenient representation of character values:

```
char digit = '9';
char w = 'w';
char newline = '\n';
char tab = '\t';
char null = '\0';
```

The character values are always positive, even when they are contained in a `signed char`. They can be used as integer operands in expressions:

```
int value = digit - '0';
```

Useful calculations on character values usually assume certain standard character sets, such as ASCII or EBCDIC.

1.2 Scalar Types with Relational and Logical Operators

There is no boolean type in C++. Scalar types, like integers, work as boolean with zero representing the value FALSE and any nonzero value representing TRUE. Pointers are also scalar types and are described later in this chapter. The relational operators are used to compare values and return TRUE or FALSE in the form of an integer value of 1 or 0. The logical operators work on scalar operands interpreted as TRUE or FALSE and likewise return 1 or 0.

Relational operators produce `int` results of either 1 or 0. The example in the previous section calculating the distance traveled during a fall uses a relational expression to control the loop.

```
for( int t = 1; t <= 10; t++ ) {
    // etc.
}
```

To highlight the control condition, we will rewrite the `for` loop as an equivalent `while` loop.

```
int t = 1;
while( t <= 10 ) {
    // etc.
    t++;
}
```

The loop body executes as long as the condition `t <= 10` does not evaluate to 0. The expression evaluates to 1 as long as t is less than or equal to 10 so the loop executes for values of t from 1 to 10.

The relational operators are less than <, greater than >, less than or equal to <= and greater than or equal to >=. There are also the equality operators equal to == and not equal to !=. These operators are overloaded for integer and floating point, as well as pointer operands, but always produce an int result of 1 or 0.

Because any nonzero value represents TRUE, any expression can serve as a condition, not just those that evaluate to 1 or 0. For example:

```
int t = 11;
while( --t ) {
    // etc.
}
```

The loop body executes for values of t from 10 to 1.

The logical operators are AND &&, OR ||, and NOT !. An expression with the unary operator ! evaluates to 0 if its operand is nonzero and 1 otherwise. For example, the following sets a previously zero valued variable:

```
if( !p )     // i.e. if( p == 0 )
    p = get_a_val();
```

Expressions using || evaluate to 0 if both operands are 0 and 1 otherwise. In the following example, the function error is called only if the value of x is not in the range 0 to 10.

```
if( x < 0 || x > 10 )
    error("value outside range");
```

An && expression evaluates to 1 if both operands are nonzero and 0 otherwise. The following checks the same condition as the previous example using a different logical expression:

```
if( !( x >= 0 && x <= 10 ) )
    error("value outside range");
```

The first expression is preferable to the second because it is easier to understand.

The second operand of && and || is evaluated only if needed to determine the result of the expression. If the first operand of an || expression evaluates to nonzero, the result is 1 regardless of the value of the second operand. Likewise, if the first operand of an && expression evaluates to 0, the second operand is not evaluated, and the result of the expression is 0. For example, in the following, if b has the value 0, the equality expression is not evaluated and the division subexpression will likewise be bypassed.

```
if( b && a/b == c ) {
    // etc.
}
```

The use of `&&` checks that b is not 0 and thus avoids the possibility of a division by 0.

1.3   Nonabstract Operations

C++ has a number of operations that allow a programmer to bypass abstract interpretations of types and get at their machine representation.

Integer types are implemented on a computer as bit sequences of different lengths. When integers are used with arithmetic, relational, or logical operators, their values are interpreted abstractly as numbers, or as TRUE or FALSE, and the details of the bit representation can be ignored by the programmer. Sometimes the programmer wants to deal with the bits, however.

Below is a string hash function originated by Peter Weinberger. A hash function calculates a numeric value from a character string and is used to determine a storage location for information keyed on the string. The parameter is a pointer to a sequence of characters that are used as numeric values in the calculation. The variable `hash` is manipulated as a sequence of 32 bits until it is used as a numeric value in taking the remainder of its division by `prime`.

```
int
hashpjw( char *s ) {
    const prime = 211;
    unsigned hash = 0, g;

    for( char *p = s; *p ; p++ ) {
        hash = ( hash << 4 ) + *p;
        // assumes 32 bit int size
        if( g = hash & 0xf0000000 ) {
            hash ^= g >> 24;
            hash ^= g;
        }
    }
    return hash % prime;
}
```

The bitwise operators used above are left shift <<, right shift >>, bitwise AND &, and bitwise exclusive OR ^. Bitwise inclusive OR | and the unary bitwise complement ~ are also available.

The ^ operator is used in the example in the form of an assignment operator ^=. The expression

```
hash ^= g;
```

is equivalent to

```
hash = hash ^ g;
```

The binary operators *, /, %, +, -, <<, >>, &, ^, and | can all be combined with assignment in the same way.

The sizeof operator gives the number of chars used to represent a type. For example the result of

```
sizeof( int )
```

is the number of bytes used to represent an int. The value of

```
sizeof( char )
```

is always 1. When the operand is an expression instead of a type, the result is the size of the type of the expression. A major use of this operator, determining of space needed for dynamic creation of an object, has been incorporated into the C++ memory management operators new and delete. With these operators taking care of the mechanics of space allocation, a programmer will rarely need to know the size of a type representation.

1.4 User-Defined Types

Class types can be defined by the user to extend the basic C++ type system. Operations and conversions can be defined for class types so that they can be used in combination with other types.

The following is a program that calculates the voltage of an AC electrical circuit containing a conductor, a resistor and a capacitor using the formula $Z = R + j\omega L + 1 / (j\omega C)$ for impedance and $V = ZI$ for voltage. The voltage, current, and impedance of AC circuits have two components that are represented by the real and imaginary parts of a complex number. There is no language-defined complex number type in C++. The program uses a user-defined class type to represent complex number values.

```
#include "complex.h"

main() {
/*
    calculate voltage of an AC circuit
*/
    const complex j( 0, 1 );    // imaginary 1
    const double pi = 3.1415926535897931;

    double
        L = .03,      // inductance, in henries
        R = 5000,     // resistance, in ohms
        C = .02,      // capacitance, in farads
        freq = 60,    // frequency in hertz
        omega = 2 * pi * freq;
                      // frequency in radians/sec
    complex
        I = 12,       // current
        Z,            // impedance
        V;            // voltage

    Z = R + j * omega * L + 1/( j * omega * C );
    V = Z * I;
    V.print();
}
```

The output of the program is

```
( 60000.00, 134.13 )
```

The header file `complex.h` contains the definition of the class type `complex`, that implements the mathematical notion of complex numbers. An abridged version of `class complex` is used for the example.

```
class complex {
    double re, im;
  public:
    complex( double r = 0, double i = 0 )
        { re = r; im = i; }
    void print();
    friend complex operator +( complex, complex );
    friend complex operator *( complex, complex );
    friend complex operator /( complex, complex );
};
```

The class definition contains the declarations of members as well as the declaration of `friend` functions, which have special access to members of the class. The members declared after the `public` label are accessible without restriction, whereas the private members, `re` and `im`, can only be accessed by member and friend functions. The data member representation of `complex` is hidden in the private part of the class, and so the type is only usable through the publicly available functions.

The member function with the same name as the class is a *constructor*. The constructor is used to create and initialize `complex` objects, or to convert values of other types to the class type. This constructor is declared with default argument values, so it can be invoked with zero, one, or two arguments, with the default arguments being filled in when needed. The declaration

```
const complex j( 0, 1 );
```

has an initializer that provides both constructor arguments, with the real and imaginary parts of `j` being set to 0 and 1, respectively. The declaration

```
complex I = 12;
```

is equivalent to

```
complex I( 12, 0 );
```

The default argument fills in 0 for the argument that sets the imaginary part of `I`. Both `Z` and `V` are initialized with the default constructor arguments, because no other initial values are indicated in their declarations.

The other functions declared in `class complex` are defined outside the class:

```
void
complex::print() {
    printf("( %5.2f, %5.2f )\n", re, im );
}

complex
operator +( complex a1, complex a2 ) {
    return complex( a1.re + a2.re, a1.im + a2.im );
}
```

```
complex
operator *( complex a1, complex a2 )
{
    return complex(a1.re * a2.re - a1.im * a2.im,
            a1.re * a2.im + a1.im * a2.re);
}


complex
operator / (complex a1, complex a2)
{
    double r = a2.re;    /* (r,i) */
    double i = a2.im;
    double ti;         /* (tr,ti) */
    double tr;

    tr = r < 0? -r : r;
    ti = i < 0? -i : i;
    if (tr <= ti) {
        ti = r/i;
        tr = i * (1 + ti*ti);
        r = a1.re;
        i = a1.im;
    }
    else {
        ti = -i/r;
        tr = r * (1 + ti*ti);
        r = -a1.im;
        i = a1.re;
    }
    return complex( (r*ti + i)/tr, (i*ti - r)/tr );
}
```

The member function `print` is used in the example to print the resulting value of V.

```
V.print();
```

As a member function, `print` can access all the other members of the class without restriction. It formats and prints the `re` and `im` members of the `complex` object for which it is called.

The operator functions are declared as `friend` inside class `complex`. Friend functions are not members of the class, but like member functions they are allowed access to private members of a `complex` object. The operator functions implement arithmetic operations for `complex` values and allow `complex` operands in expressions with infix notation.

```
Z = R + j * omega * L + 1/( j * omega * C );
```

The expression that calculates impedance mixes `int`, `double`, and `complex` operands. When an `int` or `double` operand is used with a `complex` one, the constructor is automatically applied to convert the operand to `complex` before the operator function is called with the operands as arguments. Predefined conversions between built-in types are applied to get the correct constructor argument types, so the single constructor serves to convert both `int` and `double` operands. When the `complex` constructor is used in conversions, the default value is filled in as the second argument.

With the hidden representation and user-defined operators and conversions, `class complex` is an abstract numeric type that combines naturally with the predefined numeric types.

1.5 Pointers and Arrays

Pointers and arrays are derived from other types. Pointer types represent the addresses of objects of another type. They are used to keep track of dynamically allocated objects, for flexibility in data structures, and with pointer arithmetic operators to access elements of arrays. Array types represent a sequence of elements of a particular type and have many uses as aggregate data structures. One standard use of arrays is as strings, which are sequences of characters.

Pointer types are indicated by using the type modifier * along with other type information in declarations. The same symbol is used for the pointer dereference operator, which returns the object being pointed to. The result of a dereference can be used for the value of the object or on the left-hand side of an assignment.

```
int *p;      // p is a pointer to int
int i = 33;
p = &i;      // p set to point to i
*p = *p + 1;   // i set to 34
```

The & operator returns the address of the object that is its operand. Address values have the type pointer-to-object-type.

The dynamic allocation operator `new` creates an object having a type indicated by its operand and returns a pointer to the new object. An object created by new can be destroyed using operator delete, which takes as its operand a pointer to the doomed object.

```
int *p = 0;

if( !p )
    p = new int;

delete p;
p = 0;
```

The code fragment above declares a pointer and initializes it to 0, which is the special null pointer value and an invalid address. The pointer is checked to see if it has been set, and if not, it is given the address of a newly created object. The object is then deleted, and the pointer is reset to null. The combination of pointers, the use of null pointers as flags, and the allocation and deallocation of objects with operators new and delete are the rudiments for building dynamic data structures in C++.

There are no automatic conversions among pointer types, except in limited cases in assignment and initialization. There is a special void * pointer type that will hold a pointer value of any type. One can think of void * as a pointer-to-anything type. Any other pointer type is automatically converted to match a void * in an assignment or initialization.

```
int *ip;
void *vp = ip;
double *dp;
vp = dp;
ip = (int *)vp; // not a good idea
```

A void * is only converted to another type of pointer if the programmer explicitly requests it with a cast. Such an explicit conversion is risky because it bypasses the type checking that ensures that the pointed-to object is interpreted in a consistent way. There are automatic conversions among pointers to related class types. These are discussed in Chapter 5.

An array is a sequence of contiguously allocated elements of the same type. The addresses of the elements in an array can be calculated from those of other elements using arithmetic operations overloaded for pointer operands. A loop that sequences through the elements of a string demonstrates a use of pointer arithmetic:

```
for( char *p = s; *p ; p++ ) {
    // etc.
```

In this example, s is an array of char, which represents a string. The pointer p is initialized to point to the first element in the array and then incremented to point to successive elements, until one of the elements is 0. The string is conventionally terminated by a 0 element.

Both increment ++ and decrement -- operators work on pointer operands whose values are assumed to be the addresses of array elements. Increment changes the pointer to refer to the next element in the array, and decrement changes it to refer to the previous element.

The binary operators addition + and subtraction - are defined to work on one pointer operand and one integer operand. For subtraction, the integer must be the second operand. Again, the pointers are assumed to be the addresses of array elements. The results of the operations are addresses of other array elements. For example, the following addition adjusts p to point to the third element past the one it originally pointed to.

```
p += 3;
```

The following subtraction sets p to the second element before the original one.

```
p -= 2;
```

Subtraction is also defined to work on two pointer operands that are the addresses of elements in the same array. The result is an int value that is the number of elements between the array locations referred to by the pointers.

An array type is indicated with the type modifier []. In an array declaration, the braces contain the number of elements in the array. For example

```
char buffer[100];
```

declares an array of 100 char elements. The name buffer represents the address of the first element in the array. This name can be used with the pointer arithmetic operations to access the elements of the array. The following loop zeros out the elements of buffer.

```
for( int i = 0; i < 100; i++ )
    *( buffer + i ) = 0;
```

A pointer expression can be used to access array elements. In the following, p is initially set to the address of the first element of buffer and then used to copy the first twenty elements into another array called name.

```
char name[21];

p = buffer;
for( i = 0; i< 20; i++ )
    name[i] = *p++;
```

The subscript operator [ ] provides a shorthand expression for the pointer operations used to access array elements. The subscript expression

```
name[i]
```

is the same as

```
*(name + i)
```

The subscript operator can be used with any pointer operand, not just array names. The following sets the location before p to null:

```
p[-1] = '\0';
```

The basic representation of a string in C++ is a sequence of character values in a char array with a terminating 0 element. String literals provide a way of representing such arrays. A string literal is a sequence of characters or escape sequences surrounded by double quotes:

```
"This is a string literal\n"
```

The value of a string literal is a pointer to the first element of a char array whose size is one more than the number of characters between the quotes. The array elements have the values of the characters followed by the value 0.

1.6 References

Reference types establish aliases for objects. They are used as function parameter types in order to pass arguments by reference, instead of by value.

A reference type is indicated in a declaration by using the modifier & in the same way as a pointer modifier. A reference must have an initializer. Once the reference is initialized, its use produces the same results as if the aliased object were used directly. The major use of references is for parameter types. In order to demonstrate how references work, we first show them in nonparameter declarations.

To establish an alias, the initializer should be the name of an object of the type that is referenced.

```
int i;
int &ir = i;
```

This establishes `ir` as an alias for `i`. Assignment to and use of `ir` produces the same results as assignment to and use of `i`.

```
ir = 3;      // i gets the value 3
int j;
int *ip;
j = i * ir; // j gets the value 9
ip = &ir;    // ip gets the address of i
```

Once the initializer establishes the object that the reference aliases, it cannot be changed.

If the initializer for the reference is not of the right type, an anonymous object is created for which the reference becomes an alias. The initializer is converted, and its value is used to set the value of the anonymous object.

```
double d;
int &ir = d;     // anonymous int object created
ir = 3.0;        // d is not changed!
```

An anonymous object is also created to initialize a reference when the initializer is not an object.

```
int &ir = 3;      // anonymous object gets value 3
```

A major use of reference type parameters is to allow a function to set the value of its actual arguments. In this case, references are used to establish aliases for the arguments within the function.

```
void input( int &, int &, int & );
int a, b, c;

input( a, b, c );    // set argument values
```

Pointer parameters can also be used to change objects external to the function, but address and pointer operations are then needed in manipulating arguments and parameters. Reference parameters that establish aliases provide a convenient alternative to pointer arguments.

Another use of reference parameters is to avoid the overhead of initializing parameters with argument values. This is most important for class parameters in which the argument values might actually be rather large data structures.

```
class list {
    // list of up to 100 int elements
  public:
    int size;
    int elements[100];
};
```

```
void output( list & );   // don't copy list value
```

In this example, `output` will use the `list` argument directly without copying its value, thus avoiding the overhead of reproducing the array of elements.

The creation of anonymous objects to initialize references allows conversions to be done to match arguments to reference parameters in the same way as nonreference parameters. For example, we could change our `complex` operator functions so they don't copy `complex` arguments, but still allow conversions for other numeric arguments:

```
class complex {
    // etc.
    friend complex operator *( complex &, complex & );
};
```

```
complex V, Z;
// etc.
```

```
V = Z * 12;
```

The expression `Z*12` is a call to the `complex` operator * function with the arguments `Z` and an anonymous `complex` object initialized with `12`. These objects initialize the reference parameters and so argument passing overhead is reduced without preventing conversions in mixed type expressions.

1.7 Const Qualified Types

The `const` type qualifier indicates that an object of the type cannot have its value changed, either directly or through a pointer. As we have already mentioned, this property allows a `const` to be a symbolic representation of its initializing value.

Reference parameters that are used to prevent argument copying and are not intended to change arguments can be declared `const` to ensure that they do not:

```
complex operator *( const complex &, const complex & );
```

The const prevents the actual parameters from being altered within the
function.

In a pointer declaration, the position of const indicates whether it's the
pointer or the object being pointed to that can't be changed. The qualifier
before the pointer modifier indicates the object being pointed to is const:

```
const char *p = buffer; // pointer to const char
p = name;        // ok
*p = 'x';        // error!
```

The qualifier after the modifier indicates the pointer itself cannot be
changed:

```
char * const p - buffer;    // const pointer to char
*p = 'X';           // ok
p = name;           // error!
```

The address of a const object cannot be assigned to a pointer to non-
const, because such an assignment might result in a change of the const
through the pointer.

```
const char space = ' ';
const char *p = &space; // ok
char *q = &space;       // error!
```

1.8 Exercises

Exercise 1-1. Write a C++ program that tells you how many bits are used
to represent objects of type char, short, int, and long. □

Exercise 1-2. The output produced by the following program is:

```
a 3 b 2 c 2
```

Explain why.

```
#include <stdio.h>

int f( int i ) { return ++i; }
int g( int &i ) { return ++i; }
int h( char &i ) { return ++i; }

main() {
    int a = 0, b = 0, c = 0;
    a += f( g( a ) );
    b += g( f( b ) );
    c += f( h( c ) );
    printf( " a %d b %d c %d\n", a, b, c);
}
```

☐

Exercise 1-3. †Given the declarations

```
int &a = 12;
int *b;
int *&c = b;
int *d[5];
```

what are the types of the following expressions?

```
a
b
*b
c
*c
d[2]
*d
**d
c[-2]
c-2
*(c-2)
&c
```

☐

Exercise 1-4. †Given the declarations

```
char c;
const char cc = 'a';
char *pc;
const char *pcc;
char *const cpc = &c;
const char *const cpcc = &cc;
char *const *pcpc;
```

which of the following assignments are legal, which are illegal, and why?

```
c = cc;
cc = c;
pcc = &c;
pcc = &cc;
pc = &c;
pc = &cc;
pc = pcc;
pc = cpc;
pc = cpcc;
cpc = pc;
*cpc = *pc;
pc = *pcpc;
**pcpc = *pc;
*pc = **pcpc;
```

☐

Exercise 1-5. Explain the semantics of each of the following functions:

```
void
swap1( int *a, int *b ) {
    int t = *a;
    *a = *b;
    *b = t;
}

void
swap2( int &a, int &b ) {
    int t = a;
    a = b;
    b = t;
}
```

```
void
flop( int a, int b ) {
    int t;
    t = a;
    a = b;
    b = t;
}
```

□

Exercise 1-6. Run the following program.

```
#include <stdio.h>

int &
f() {
    int i = 1;
    return i;
}

int
g() {
    int j = 2;
    return j;
}

main() {
    int &ri = f();
    g();
    printf( "%d\n", ri );
}
```

What output does it produce on your system? Explain why. □

CHAPTER 2: **Procedural Programming**

A program is a sequence of operations on data structures that implements an algorithm or procedure to solve a problem. For most problems, the procedure is long and complicated enough that a program is difficult to implement and costly to maintain without methods for managing its size and complexity. Procedural programming techniques provide methods for dividing and structuring programs so that they are easy to build, understand, and maintain. These techniques focus on organizing the sequence of operations in the program and for the most part ignore the data structures on which the operations are performed.

In C++, a program starts execution with the `main` function, after the initialization of static data structures. Practically, `main` never contains all the operations in the program, for some are always delegated to other functions, or built into the data structures using features that are presented in Chapter 3. In this chapter, we will use only simple forms of data structures and cover the use of procedural programming techniques in designing and organizing the functions in a C++ program.

2.1 Functions as Modules

A function is a module that encapsulates a sequence of operations. Functions have parameters so that their operations are generalized to apply to any actual arguments of the right type. The inputs to a function are the arguments and the global data objects that are used in the function. The results are its return value, modifications made through pointer and reference arguments, and changes to global data.

The inputs and results are the interface to the function module. Users need only understand this interface to use the function. The actual sequence of operations that implements the function is a hidden detail, so the function can be considered a single abstract operation. Designing and implementing

29

the functions in a program can be thought of as building special operations that solve a given problem.

Programs must not only satisfy technical goals of correctly solving a problem but must also satisfy economic goals of being affordable. The modularity of functions can be used to make them more understandable and reusable, and therefore help reduce the cost of program implementation and maintenance.

Functions are easy to understand if they are designed to correspond to abstract operations needed in a solution. The function, and its use in the program, can then be thought of in terms of the problem, and not in the details of the implementation. For example, a function that takes as input an unsorted list and reorders the elements in ascending order, might be described as the abstract operation ''sort a list.'' The same abstract operation might be part of many problem solutions. The function that implements the operation might also be used in many programs if it is designed to be independent of its context in a program.

A function that does not use global data objects has only parameterized input. Instead of operating on a particular object given in the program, the function is an operation on any arguments of the correct type. The function can be reused with different inputs not only in the original program, but also in other programs with the same type of data structures. The interface can be understood from its declaration, and the data object references in its implementation can be understood from declarations local to the function. With the parameterized input and locality of reference, the function is an easily reusable, somewhat self-documenting module.

2.2 Functional Decomposition

Functional decomposition is a method for subdividing a large program into functions. Starting with an overall description of what the program is to do, the method decomposes the action into a number of steps or abstract operations. Each step is implemented as a function in the program. Any function can itself be refined into substeps that can be implemented as functions. Finally, a level of detail is achieved when the steps can be implemented without functions.

This design method results in a hierarchy of functions in which higher-level functions delegate work to lower-level functions. This method is also known as top-down design, because it starts at a high-level description of the program, then works through the refinement of the design to the low-level details of the implementation.

As an example, let us consider a program to sort a list of words. First we need to represent the list and the words in the program. The data structure for words are character strings, null-terminated sequences of characters accessed by pointers. The list is represented by an array containing pointers to the strings. This array has a maximum size and a size indicating how many strings have been entered into the array.

We give the `char *` string type a name using a `typedef` declaration, then set up the list and initialize it as empty.

```
typedef char *String;

const int max = 100;
String list[max];
int size = 0;
```

We are now ready to design the functions in our program. The problem is to take a list and produce a sorted list. At the highest level, this can be broken down into three operations:

```
read the original list
sort the list
print out the sorted list
```

We have three functions that are called from the `main` function in our program:

```
int input( String *, int );
void sort( String *, int );
void output ( String *, int );

main() {
    size = input( list, max );
    sort( list, size );
    output( list, size );
}
```

Up to the maximum size of the list, `input` reads strings and enters them into the list, and returns the size of the list; `sort` puts the list elements in order; and `output` prints out each string in the list. Notice that the array and size information have been made parameters of the functions. The functions are only used once in this program and could have accessed the global data directly instead of passing it as arguments. In this program, benefits of parameterized functions would come from easier maintenance and reuse of the functions in other programs.

The input, sort, and output functions are straightforward, except for reading and printing strings, and the comparison of strings needed to do the sort. We delegate these tasks to lower-level functions and will not discuss them until later.

```
int readString( String & );
void printString( String );
int lessthan( String, String );


int
input( String *a, int limit ) {
    for( int i = 0; i < limit ; i++ )
        if( !readString( a[i] ) )
            break;
    return i;
}

void
output ( String *a, int size ) {
    for( int i = 0; i < size; i++ )
        printString( a[i] );
}


void
sort( String *a, int n ) {
    // this uses a bubble sort algorithm
    int changed;
    do {
        changed = 0;
        for( int i = 0; i < n-1 ; i++ )
            if( lessthan( a[i+1], a[i] ) ) {
                String temp = a[i];
                a[i] = a[i+1];
                a[i+1] = temp;
                changed = 1;
            }
    } while( changed );
}
```

If it reads a string, `readString` returns 1 and 0 if it fails. The function `lessthan` returns 1 if the first argument is lexically less than the second, and 0 otherwise.

Finally, we come to the functions that do the exact work on the strings. The functions we need are already available in standard libraries.

```
#include <stdio.h>
#include <string.h>

int
readString( String &s ) {
    // read a string and copy it into
    // its own space, remembering to add
    // space for the terminating null

    const bufsize = 100;
    static char buffer[bufsize];

    if( scanf( "%s", buffer ) == EOF )
        return 0;
    s = new char[ strlen(buffer)+1 ];
    if( !s )      // new fails
        return 0;
    strcpy( s, buffer );
    return 1;
}

void
printString( String s ) {
    printf(" %s", s );
}


int
lessthan( String s1, String s2 ) {
    return strcmp( s1, s2 ) < 0;
}
```

The function `readString` has a reference argument because it is meant to set the value of its argument to the newly created string. If a `String` instead of a `String &` argument type were used, the assignment to s would only set its local value, without changing the value of the actual argument provided in the function call. The reference type lets the actual argument be set inside the function through the alias of the parameter name.

Note that `scanf` and `printf` do the string input and output and are declared in the standard library header file `stdio.h`. In addition, `scanf` returns a value `EOF` when it reaches the end of a file, and `strlen` gives the number of characters in a string, excluding the terminating `'\0'`. Finally, `strcpy` copies one string to another and `strcmp` returns 0 if the strings have the same characters, or a negative or positive value depending on whether the first argument comes lexically before or after the second.

These functions are declared in `string.h`.

The top-down design of this program is represented by a hierarchical diagram:

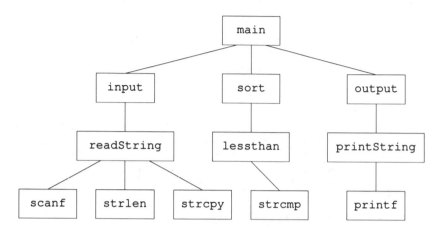

2.3 File Organization

The unit of compilation in C++ is the file. Any number of C++ files can be compiled and linked together to form an executable program. Declarations and definitions with *external linkage* allow cross-file reference of functions and data. The usual way of providing access to the external definitions in a file is to create a separate *header file* that contains the external declarations and supporting type definitions needed to use the functions and objects in the file correctly. The declarations in the header file are then included in any file that uses the external functions or objects. Functions and global objects declared as `static` have *internal linkage* and cannot be referenced outside the file in which they are declared. Global objects declared as `const` also have internal linkage unless explicitly declared `extern`.

Separating a large program into files can ease the process of developing, understanding, and maintaining a program. For example, a number of programmers can work on the same program simultaneously without interfering with one another; related functions and data structures can be grouped together to make them easy to read and understand; and local modifications can be made with limited external effect.

Code separated out into a file is also easier to pick up for reuse in another program. This is the typical way code is reused, for example, as in libraries. We have already shown the use of the standard input/output and string libraries. The functions declared in `stdio.h` and `string.h` are provided in publicly available files. The client code links to these libraries to form the complete program.

Because we designed the string-array functions in our example to be general, we will reorganize our list sort program and put the functions into a file that can be used in other programs.

We put the `main` function in a file called `main.c`. A `.c` at the end of a file name is the convention we use to indicate that it contains C++ program text. File naming conventions differ in various C++ programming environments.

```
#include "strarray.h"

const int max = 100;
String list[max];

int size = 0;

main() {
    size = input( list, max );
    sort( list, size );
    output( list, size );
}
```

When `main.c` is compiled, the contents of file `strarray.h` are inserted into the text at the `#include`. `strarray.h` contains the declarations needed to use the string-array functions:

```
typedef char *String;

int input( String *, int );
void sort( String *, int );
void output ( String *, int );
```

The definitions of the functions declared in `strarray.h` are put in `strarray.c`. In rearranging our functions, we have also gotten rid of `printString` because it did not add anything to the operation already provided by `printf`.

```
#include <stdio.h>
#include <string.h>
#include "strarray.h"

static int
readString( String &s ) {
    // nothing new
}

static int
lessthan( String s1, String s2 ) {
    // nothing new
}


int
input( String *a, int limit ) {
    // nothing new
}

void
output( String *a, int size ) {
    for( int i = 0; i < size; i++ )
        printf( " %s", a[i] );
}

void
sort( String *a, int n ) {
    // nothing new
}
```

Along with the standard headers that declare the library functions used in the implementation, strarray.c includes its interface header strarray.h. This is done to get the needed type definition of String and as a consistency check between the declarations and implementations. If the declaration in the header did not agree with the function definitions, the source file would not compile.

Notice that the auxiliary functions readString and lessthan have been declared static, indicating that they have internal linkage and cannot be accessed from other files. Because their use is restricted to this file, they can be changed, or even deleted, according to modifications needed by functions in this file without affecting external users.

2.4 Structured Programming

The use of structured programming techniques helps to make a function implementation easy to understand. The methods include using regular control structures, partitioning the function into blocks, formatting, and annotating the code with comments.

Control statements allow branches and loops to be implemented in such a way that the flow of control in a function can be followed easily. The statements give control structures regular, easily recognizable forms. C++ control statements are branches: `if`, `if-else`, `switch`; and loops: `for`, `while`, `do-while`. There are also a number of jump statements: `break`, for jumping out of loops and switches; `continue`, for progressing to the next loop iteration; `return`, for function return; and the infamous `goto`. Because of its generality in allowing jumps to anywhere in a function, a `goto` can make the sequence of operations in the function hard to follow and understand. Any use of a `goto` should be examined to see if it can be recoded using branch or loop statements.

Jumps can create problems not only because they obscure the flow of control. It is illegal for control to jump over a declaration with an initializer into the scope of that declaration, either with a `goto`:

```
    goto label;
    int i = 3;   // Error!
label:
    i++;
```

or in a control structure:

```
switch( x ) {
    int i = 0;   // Wrong!
case 1: {
    int j = 1;   // Ok.
    break;
}
case 2:
    // etc.
default:
    break;
}
```

The only correct way to jump over a declaration with an initializer is to bypass the entire scope of the declaration.

All functions contain at least the block that is their body, and the function parameter declarations are considered to be within that block. Blocks can be nested within other blocks.

Most often, blocks are used to group collections of statements within control structures. They can also be used to localize names that have limited use, however. For example, in the `sort` function, `temp` is declared within the block in which it is used.

```
if( lessthan( a[i+1], a[i] ) ) {
    String temp = a[i];
    // etc.
}
```

The local variable is initialized when the flow of control passes its point of declaration and goes out of existence when control leaves the block immediately enclosing the declaration. If `temp` were declared at an outer block, its purpose would not be so clearly understood from the context of its declaration, and there would be no useful initializing value available. Keeping the declaration at local block scope also allows the common, mnemonic name to be reused in other scopes.

Declarations are statements and can appear any place a statement can within a block. This flexibility allows names to be declared and initialized at the point of their first use. For example, the first clause in a `for` loop control is a statement so a loop index can be declared there.

```
for( int i = 0; i < limit ; i++ )  {
    // etc.
}
return i;
```

The scope of a name extends from its point of declaration to the end of its block. Notice that in this example, `i` is still available after the loop terminates. It goes out of scope at the end of the block that contains the `for` statement.

Formatting conventions are important for making a function readable. Most important for conveying the control structure of the function is the use of indentation to indicate the nesting of statements and blocks. Also, commonly sought sections of text should be easy to find. For example, declarations, the beginning and end of function blocks, and labels should be clearly visible. Code sections can be highlighted by different indentation levels, surrounding white space, and position at the start of a line or the beginning of a block. Comments can also be used to mark sections of code.

There are two ways to separate comments from code in C++. Block comments start with /* and end with */, and line comments start with // and go to the end of the line. Comments can be used to give overview explanations of functions or complicated sections of code. They can also explain statements with subtle or hidden implications. For example, hidden order dependencies between operations should be pointed out as well as assumptions on which the implementation is based.

```
/*
      The global variable flag1 must be set
      before the call to func1 because it sets
      the context for the later call to func2
*/


//   Assumes ASCII Character Set
```

Comments also should be used in noting irregularities. For example, a comment like

```
// this is a kludge
```

points out an irregular bug fix in the program, although it is not very helpful. It is better to make the comment informative:

```
// ad hoc correction of roundoff error
```

Perhaps the most important way of commenting a function is to choose function and variable names that make their use self-explanatory. In particular, function names should convey the meaning of the abstract operation that the function implements, as in the above example with input, sort, and output. If meaningful and mnemonic names are used in a program, there is often only occasional need for additional comments. If meaningful names are not used, it is unlikely that any added comments will make the code easy to understand.

The previous discussion assumes that the programmer wants to help others understand his or her program. A program can be written to solve a problem without consideration for future use, or, in order to keep others from changing or reusing the program, it can be deliberately made to be obscure. The tactics of removing comments and formatting, as well as substituting names, are often used to make stealing code very costly for competitors. Other than for overt acts of hostility, however, writing obscure code and leaving out comments are bad ideas. Most programs eventually require maintenance, whether or not they are maintainable. Programs that are difficult to understand are hard to update without causing damage with the change. The cost of maintenance will accumulate or the program will have to be discarded. To prolong the usefulness of their work, programmers should make their programs understandable.

2.5 Overloading and Inline Functions

We have discussed how functions can be used as implementations of abstract operations, and how function names document the operations. This use is further supported by the features of *overloaded* and *inline* functions.

Overloading allows the same name to be used for different function implementations, as long as the implementations can be distinguished by the type or number of their parameters. In this way the same abstract operation can be implemented on different types of operands without concocting artificial names to differentiate the functions.

For example, we can overload `sort` to work on two types of lists.

```
typedef char *String;

void sort( String *, int );
void sort( int *, int );
```

In old versions of C++, an explicit declaration

```
overload sort;
```

is needed before the function can be overloaded.

The first instance sorts an array of strings, the second sorts an array of integers. The function call

```
sort( list, size );
```

invokes the first instance if `list` has type `String *` or the second instance if it has type `int *`.

Inline functions support the use of small functions when, for reasons of efficiency, a programmer is reluctant to use a function call to invoke the few statements that implement an abstract operation. The specifier `inline` on a function declaration is a hint to the compiler to optimize a call to that function with an inline expansion of the function body. Inline expansion does not change the semantics of the function call. Any function may be declared inline, but the optimization of the function call may not always be done, depending on the capabilities of the compiler and how the call is made. Like a function declared `static`, an inline function can be used only in the file in which it is defined, because the definition must be visible at the point of call for the optimization to be possible. For an inline function to be used across files, it should be included in a header file.

In our example, the string comparison operator `lessthan` is a natural candidate for an inline function, because it contains only a single statement.

```
inline int
lessthan( String s1, String s2 ) {
    return strcmp( s1, s2 ) < 0 ;
}
```

Below we use both function overloading and the inline `lessthan` in an
extended version of our list-sort example, which first sorts a list of strings,
then a list of numbers. The lists are again implemented as arrays, but now
there are two arrays with different types of elements.

```
#include "arrays.h"

const int max = 100;
String stringlist[max];
int intlist[max];

int size = 0;

main() {
    // Read, sort, and write a list of words
    size = input( stringlist, max );
    sort( stringlist, size );
    output( stringlist, size );

    // Read, sort, and write a list of numbers
    size = input( intlist, max );
    sort( intlist, size );
    output( intlist, size );
}
```

The header file `arrays.h` contains the declarations of the overloaded
array functions.

```
typedef char* String;

overload input, output, sort;

void input( String *, const int, int & );
void input( int *, const int, int & );

void output( String *, const int );
void output( int *, const int );

void sort( String *, const int );
void sort( int *, const int );
```

The functions are provided in `arrays.c`. The full implementation of both versions of the overloaded functions is presented to show that they are almost duplicates. This demonstrates another kind of function reuse: reuse by stealing code and editing. To put it another way, a generic function-text template was used for both functions, and simple text substitutions were used to make the necessary type differentiations. More sophisticated methods of copying and editing code are discussed in Chapter 4.

```
#include <stdio.h>
#include <string.h>
#include "arrays.h"

static int
readString( String &s ) {
    // nothing new, see above
}

inline int
lessthan( String s1, String s2 ) {
    return strcmp( s1, s2 ) < 0 ;
}

int
input( String *a, int limit ) {
    for( int i = 0; i < limit ; i++ )
        if( !readString( a[i] ) )
            break;
    return i;
}

int
input( int *a, int limit ) {
    for( int i = 0; i < limit ; i++ )
        if( scanf( "%d", a+i ) == EOF )
            break;
    return i;
}

void
output( String *a, int size ) {
    printf( "\nlist:" );
    for( int i = 0; i < size; i++ )
        printf( " %s", a[i] );
    printf("\n");
}
```

```
void
output( int *a, int size ) {
    printf( "\nlist:" );
    for( int i = 0; i < size; i++ )
        printf( " %d", a[i] );
    printf( "\n" );
}

void
sort( String *a, int n ) {
    int changed;
    do {
        changed = 0;
        for( int i = 0; i < n-1 ; i++ )
            if( lessthan( a[i+1], a[i] ) ) {
                String temp = a[i];
                a[i] = a[i+1];
                a[i+1] = temp;
                changed = 1;
            }
    } while( changed );
}


void
sort( int *a, int n ) {
    int changed;
    do {
        changed = 0;
        for( int i = 0; i < n-1 ; i++ )
            if( a[i+1] < a[i] ) {
                int temp = a[i];
                a[i] = a[i+1];
                a[i+1] = temp;
                changed = 1;
            }
    } while( changed );
}
```

A warning needs to be given on the use of overloaded functions. Over-loading conceptually unifies different functions in a program, but it does so by introducing ambiguity to the function name. In the overloaded sort ex-ample it is not too difficult to identify the function called by

```
sort( list, size );
```

Because there are no automatic conversions that result in the argument types, the type given by the declarations of `list` directly indicates which of the two functions is to be invoked. Given a multiply overloaded function name, and a number of conversions among possible argument types, however, the identification of the function can become complicated. The positive use of overloading to convey conceptual unity must be balanced with the negative results of having ambiguous names obscure what the program actually does.

2.6 Arguments and Return Values

A function type consists of both its parameter types and return type. In a call, the function to be called is first identified by its name. Then the identification is verified by whether the arguments in the call match the declared parameter types or can be made to match through available conversions. The choice among overloaded function instances is made by matching argument types to parameter types.

Functions that take arbitrary numbers and types of arguments have their types specified with an ellipsis in the parameter list.

```
void error( const char * ... );
```

This declaration declares `error` to be a function returning no value, taking a string first argument and any number and type of additional arguments. The `const` indicates that the string cannot be changed through the pointer, so string literals can be safely used in a call. Presumably, the first argument in a call to `error` will contain the information needed to interpret later arguments.

Arguments are automatically converted to the parameter types in a function call. If the conversion is to a class type parameter, a predefined conversion might first be applied to match the argument to the type needed by the user-defined class constructor, as was shown in the `class complex` example in Chapter 1. If the conversion is from a class type argument to a nonclass parameter type, an additional predefined conversion might be applied after the user-defined one. For arguments that match an ellipsis parameter specification, integer types are converted to `int` and floating point types are converted to `double`, but otherwise no argument conversions are applied.

When a function is executed, the formal parameters in a function definition are initialized with the actual arguments of the function call. When a value is returned from a function, it is used to initialize the result. The fact that arguments and return values are initialized, rather than assigned, is especially important for `const` and reference types, as well as class types with constructors, in which initialization is significantly different from assignment.

The formal parameters of a function are local variables within the function block. After being initialized by a function call, they can be used like any other variable, including being assigned to and having their value changed. A `const` specifier means that the declared object *cannot* have its value changed after initialization. A `const` parameter will not be altered from the original value passed as an argument. Such a parameter declaration can prevent erroneous changes to what should be fixed values. For example, in our list sort, the size of the list to be sorted is fixed. To indicate this, the parameter could have been declared `const`.

```
sort( String *, const int );
```

Except for reference parameters, formal parameters are different objects from the actual arguments. Once they are initialized with the values of the arguments, they can be used and assigned locally without any effect external to the function. As discussed in Chapter 1, reference parameters are *not* separate objects from the actual arguments. Their initialization establishes the reference name as an alias for the object that is the initializer. Reference type parameters allow "call by reference," in which an assignment to the parameter inside the function results in a change of the value of the actual argument. A reference type was used for a parameter of `readString` because the string was returned through the argument.

```
int readString( String & );
```

A convenience feature in C++ that allows flexibility in the use of functions is *default argument initializers*. Default argument values can be given in a function declaration, and are automatically supplied to function calls that have fewer than the declared number of arguments. For example, a function declared with three arguments, two with default initializers:

```
error( const char *msg, int level = 0, int kill = 0 );
```

can be called with one, two, or three arguments.

```
error( "you goofed" );
    // actual call: error( "you goofed", 0, 0 );
error( "you screwed up", 1 );
    // actual call: error( "you screwed up", 1, 0 );
error( "you blew it!", 3, 1 );
    // no default arguments used
```

Default arguments are particularly useful in minimizing the effects of changes to a program during maintenance. An existing function can be changed by adding arguments without having to alter existing function calls. A declaration with a default argument initializer for the new parameter will allow the old calls to exist as before. This makes it easier to extend the behavior of a function.

As an example, we will change our string-array sort function to sort the list in either alphabetical order or reverse. First, in our header file, we add an argument type and default initializer to the function declaration.

```
void sort( String *, int, int descending = 0 );
```

The dummy argument name in the function declaration is not needed, except as a comment to give the reader a clue about why the argument is there. When files using the header are recompiled, a third argument of 0 will be automatically added to all calls of the string-array sort function, which have only two arguments.

Now we adapt the sort function to use the new third argument. First, we add a greaterthan function that compares two strings. Then sort is changed to use a pointer-to-function variable to call either lessthan or greaterthan. The inline specifier has no optimizing effect here because the function call is through a pointer.

```
inline int
lessthan( String s1, String s2 ) {
    return strcmp( s1, s2 ) < 0 ;
}

inline int
greaterthan( String s1, String s2 ) {
    return strcmp( s1, s2 ) > 0 ;
}

void
sort( String *a, int n, int descending ) {

    int changed;
    typedef int ( * Fptype )( String, String );

    // declare and initialize pointer to comparison function
    Fptype compare = descending ?
                &greaterthan : &lessthan;

    do {
        changed = 0;
        for( int i = 0; i < n-1 ; i++ )
            if( compare( a[i+1], a[i] ) ) {
                String temp = a[i];
                a[i] = a[i+1];
                a[i+1] = temp;
                changed = 1;
            }
    } while( changed );
}
```

The ?: operator that is used to select the comparison function is a conditional expression. If the first operand descending has a nonzero value, the second operand &greaterthan is evaluated and is the result of the expression. If descending is zero, the third operand &lessthan is evaluated and is the result of the expression.

The string-array function has been extended without affecting any existing usage of the function, except for the required recompilation of the files that include the changed header. New calls to sort can take advantage of its new functionality by setting its third argument.

```
#include "arrays.h"

const int max = 100;
String stringlist[max];

int size = 0;
const int descending = 1;

main() {
    // Same as before
    size = input( stringlist, max );
    sort( stringlist, size );
    output( stringlist, size );

    // Now, into descending order
    size = input( stringlist, max );
    sort( stringlist, size, descending );
    output( stringlist, size );
}
```

2.7 Exercises

Exercise 2-1. Modify the string-sort program to be able to handle an arbitrary number of strings. Do not change the number or hierarchical relationships of the functions in your solution from that of the original solution. Is this a different solution to the problem or merely another version of the same solution? □

Exercise 2-2. Find another decomposition that solves the string-sort problem corresponding to the following conceptualization:

```
while read a string
    insert the string in sorted position
print the strings
```

Which solution is more efficient? Which solution is more easily adapted to interactive use? Which solution is better? □

Exercise 2-3. Often certain functions may be generally useful to other functions in a program. For example, an error function may be used when ever an error message is to be output, or a lookup function may used by any function needing to access stored information. How does the functional decomposition method, which produces a hierarchical design, hinder the identification of general utility functions? □

Exercise 2-4. †A token is a word or other significant group of characters in a text that is surrounded by separator characters like space, tab, or newline. Write a function that returns the address of the next token in its argument string, while modifying the value of its argument to point one character past the end of the token. Include an optional second argument to the function that specifies what characters are considered to separate tokens. Use the function to write a version of strlen, a function that returns the length of its argument string. □

Exercise 2-5. Write a function,

```
int bsearch( int *arry, int key, int num );
```

that performs a binary search for an integer key in a sorted array of integers. Rewrite bsearch to work with a) an array of doubles with a double key, b) an array of structures with an int key, c) an array of structures with a character string key, d) an array of pointers to structures with an int key, and e) an array of structures on disk, too large to read into memory in its entirety, with an int key. □

CHAPTER 3: **Classes**

Functions and the data structures on which they operate are interdependent. Functions are designed to operate on particular data structures that in turn must be left in a correct state by the functions that use them. In the string-sort example in Chapter 2, the functions depend on the data structure that represents a string to be a null-terminated character array. If one of the functions erroneously overwrote the terminating null, other functions would not work correctly on the corrupted data structure. If the representation of the string were changed to a structure containing explicit length information instead of a terminating character, a new set of functions would have to be written to work on this new data structure. Dependencies among many functions and complicated data structures can be difficult to manage in large programs.

In C++, classes support a variety of ways of organizing programs and controlling dependencies among data structures and functions. Programming techniques using classes will be the subject of the rest of this book. To lay the groundwork for later discussion, this chapter introduces the features of C++ classes.

3.1 Class Types

Classes are user-defined aggregate data types. They may contain both data members representing the type and function members that implement operations on the type. Parts of the class can either be hidden or made explicitly available by use of `private` and `public` sections of the class. Members in `private` sections can be accessed only by member functions of that class or by other functions declared to be `friend` of the class. By using this information-hiding mechanism, a class can encapsulate a data structure so that only functions specified by the class can use it.

Here we reimplement the string-sort example using a class `String` type to represent strings. The class tag `String` is a type name for the class and can be used the same way as a `typedef` name.

```
#include <stdio.h>
#include <string.h>

class String {
    char *str;
  public:
    String() { str = new char[1]; *str = 0; }
    String( char * );
    void print() { printf( " %s", str ); }
    friend int operator < ( String s1, String s2 )
        { return strcmp( s1.str, s2.str ) < 0; }
};
```

The underlying data structure used to represent a string has not changed: it is still a pointer to a null-terminated array of characters. Now, however, this structure is hidden as the member `str` in the private section of `String`. Only the `String` constructors, the member function `print`, and the friend function `operator <` can access the string representation. All the member functions are declared in the public section of the class and so are generally available for use.

The first two member functions have the same name as the class, which identifies them as *constructors* for the class. Whenever a `String` is created, a constructor is used to initialize it. The first `String` constructor takes no arguments and initializes `str` to point to an empty string. Operator `new` is used to allocate space to store the string. Because this function is short, its body is defined inside the class definition. This is a shorthand way of making a member or friend function `inline`.

The second constructor is only declared inside the class, so its definition must be provided elsewhere.

```
String::String( char *s ) {
    str = new char[ strlen(s)+1 ];
    strcpy( str, s );
}
```

In a member function definition outside of the class, the function name must be qualified to indicate that the function referred to is within the scope of the class. Here, the scope qualifier `String::` indicates that this is the definition of a `String` member.

Member functions are always within the scope of their class. Because of this, the members of the class object on which a member function is operating can be referred to without a member access operator. Note that

`String` and `print` refer to `str` without qualification. By contrast, the friend function

```
friend int operator < ( String s1, String s2 )
    { return strcmp( s1.str, s2.str ) < 0; }
```

must use the member access operator `.` to get the `str` of its arguments. Friend status makes the private member `str` accessible without error, but the function remains at the same scope it would be if it weren't a friend.

Operator functions are a way of overloading the language-defined operators to apply to class type operands. Here the less than operator has been defined to compare two `String` reference arguments. The infix operator `<` can now be used to compare two `String` operands.

Completing the string-sort example, we can see how the `String` type can be used. In the function that reads strings into the list, a constructor is used to create a `class String` object from the characters in the input buffer. This `String` object is then assigned to a slot in the list array.

```
void
input( String *a, int limit, int &i ) {
    static char buffer[100];
    for( i = 0; i < limit; i++ )
        if( scanf( "%s", buffer ) == EOF )
            break;
        else
            a[i] = String( buffer );
}
```

In the procedure that outputs the list, the `String` output function `print` is called on every element in the list using the `.` member access operator.

```
void
output( String *a, int size ) {
    printf( "\nlist: " );
    for( int i = 0; i < size; i++ )
        a[i].print();
    printf( "\n" );
}
```

In the function that sorts the list, `operator <` is invoked using infix notation to compare elements in the list, making this procedure look exactly like the sort on the integer list in Chapter 2, except for the types of the list elements.

```
void
sort( String *a, int n ) {
    int changed;
    do {
        changed = 0;
        for( int i = 0; i < n-1; i++ )
            if( a[i+1] < a[i] ) {
                String temp = a[i];
                a[i] = a[i+1];
                a[i+1] = temp;
                changed = 1;
            }
    } while( changed );
}
```

Finally, the `main` function reads, sorts, and outputs the list.

```
const int max = 10;
String list[max];

int size = 0;

main() {
    input( list, max, size );
    sort( list, size );
    output( list, size );
}
```

This looks exactly the same as the version in Chapter 2 that used a `char *` implementation of type `String`. There is a difference, however. In this case, the constructor with no arguments is called to initialize each element of `list`. The list array starts off with each element representing a proper `String` instead of being initialized to zeros. Although it doesn't matter for this program, automatic initialization of class objects through constructors makes program correctness more likely because the data structures encapsulated in the object automatically start off in a correct state.

3.2 Data Members

The definition of a class type, like that of `String` in the previous section, serves as a template for objects of the class type. When a class type object is created, space is allocated for the object and instances of the data members are created and initialized as components of the object. Like other data objects in C++, objects of class type can be created in different scopes and exist for different durations. File scope or local `static` objects are created before the start of the program execution and exist until the program ends; parameters and local objects are created when program execution reaches the point of their declaration, and remain in existence until the block in which they are declared is exited; objects created dynamically using operator `new` exist until they are explicitly destroyed using operator `delete`. Temporary objects are also created to hold intermediate results of expression evaluation and function return values.

Component members of a class object can be accessed with the member access operators `.` and `->`. The `.` operator is used with class objects.

```
String s;
s.str;
```

The `->` operator is used with pointers to class objects.

```
String *sp = new String;
sp->str;
```

The `new` operator creates an object of the type specified by its argument and returns a pointer to the new object.

Class data member types can be of any of the language-defined types, a previously defined class type, a pointer to a class type, or a reference to a class type. Pointers or references to a class type do not need to have that class defined but only need to have the class name declared. For example:

```
class Node; // declare the name only
Node *np;   // use it to declare a pointer
```

By using a pointer or a reference to the class type as a member of the class, it is possible to build recursive class structures. For example, a binary tree node would contain pointers to its left and right children.

```
class Node {
    Node *left, *right;
    // etc.
};
```

Note that these have to be pointers; a `Node` cannot contain a `Node` directly.

Each data member instance in a class object is allocated the amount of space needed to represent its type. There might be padding between members of a class object depending on the alignment needs of different machines.

One way of saving space in a class object is to use the same space for more than one member. There is a type of class in which data members are not allocated sequentially, but overlap, all starting at the initial location in the object. This kind of class is called a union. The union specifier replaces class in a declaration of a union type. Members of a union type are all public.

```
union un_type {
    int i;
    double d;
    char *p;
};
```

When a union type object is instantiated, its size and alignment is adjusted so that all the members occupy the same location in the object. The union members can be referenced using the member access operators. The result of accessing a union member is that the one location is interpreted according to the member type.

```
un_type u;

u.i = 1;       // int value stored in u
u.d = 3.1415;   // double value overwrites int value

char c = *u.p   // danger! probably bad pointer value
```

There is some peril in storing union members as one type and accessing them as another. A legal value for one member need not be legal for a different member. For correct uses of unions, there usually needs to be information available to indicate which member to use. Unions can be made members of classes when other members provide information on how to interpret the union member.

```
enum { ISINT, ISDOUBLE, ISCHARSTAR };

class Node {
    Node *left, *right;
  public:
    int code;
    un_type info;
} *np;
```

In the example, the `code` in a `Node` object will indicate how to interpret the union member

```
int i = 0; double d = 0; char *p = 0;

switch( np->code ) {
    case ISCHARSTAR:
        p = np->info.p;
        break;
    case ISDOUBLE:
        d = np->info.d;
        break;
    case ISINT:
        i = np->info.i;
        break;
}
```

Because a `Node` contains only one type of information at a time, using a union to overlap the different type members saves space in a `Node` object.

Class members can be made to overlap in a similar way without the added notation of an explicit union member access by nesting an *anonymous union* in a class. An anonymous union has no tag and declares no member name.

```
class Node {
    Node *left, *right;
  public:
    int code;
    union {
        int i;
        double d;
        char *p;
    };
} *np;
```

Here, `i`, `d`, and `p` are still allocated to overlap, but they can be accessed directly as members of `Node`.

```
int i = 0; double d = 0; char *p = 0;

switch( np->code ) {
    case ISCHARSTAR:
        p = np->p;
        break;
    case ISDOUBLE:
        d = np->d;
        break;
    case ISINT:
        i = np->i;
        break;
}
```

Another way to save space in a class object is to subdivide an integer sized segment into a number of integer type data members each using a specific number of bits. *Bitfields* allow some control over space used in a class object when it is known that certain integral members will only take a small range of values. A bitfield may be specified by following the declaration of a data member with a colon and the size of the field.

```
class Node {
    Node *left, *right;
public:
    unsigned int code: 2;
    unsigned int is_leaf: 1;
    unsigned int is_free: 1;
};
```

In the example above, `code` is allocated two bits in a `Node` object and can take on four values. The members `is_leaf` and `is_free` each have one bit, and serve as two valued flags. The fields are grouped together so that they are packed in the same segment of the object.

A programmer may be able to control the size of a class with bitfields and by grouping members to pack the space used in objects. The benefits of this control are implementation dependent. A programmer must be familiar with the sizes and alignments of types on the target machine in order to use this control successfully to save space in class objects.

Data members declared `static` are shared by all objects of the class type. A `static` member is created when the class is defined and exists before there are any class objects. It can be referenced like a data member, or without a class type object using the scope access operator `::`. Because `static` data members are independent of any particular class object, they can have their addresses taken and have pointers set to them like any other object with `static` storage duration.

As an example of a `static` data member, let's suppose we wanted to keep track of how many instances of `class String` have been created. To keep count, a `static` member of `String` is incremented by each constructor.

```
class String {
    char *str;
    static int count;
  public:
    String() { count++; str = new char; *str = 0; }
    String( char *s ) {
        count++;
        str = new char[ strlen(s)+1 ];
        strcpy( str, s );
    }
    friend void report();
    // etc.
}
```

The single instance of the static member `count` is incremented for each `string` object initialized with a constructor. To find out how many `String` type objects have been created at any point in the program, a function with the proper access permission could find out by referencing `String::count`, as in `report` below.

```
void report() {
    printf( "Report on String Usage:" );
    printf( " %d Strings created\n", String::count );
}
```

A convenience provided for using classes is that `enum` lists can be nested within a class so that the symbolic values they define are within the scope of the class. The nested `enum` values can be accessed as members of the class or by using the scope operator.

```
class Node {
    Node *left, *right;
  public:
    enum { ISINT, ISDOUBLE, ISCHARSTAR };
    int code;
    union {
        int i;
        double d;
        char *p;
    };
} *np;
```

In this example, enum values are local to the class. They do not conflict with names at different scopes, and access to them could be restricted by putting them in the private section. The class scope enum values can be referenced in the same way as static members.

```
switch( np->code ) {
    case Node::ISCHARSTAR:
        p = np->p;
        break;
    case Node::ISDOUBLE:
        d = np->d;
        break;
    case Node::ISINT:
        i = np->i;
        break;
}
```

3.3 Function Members

A function declared within a class definition and not specified as friend is a member function of that class. A member function can be defined within its class, in which case it is implicitly inline. The member access operators . and -> are used in member function calls. The . operator is used with class objects.

```
String s;
s.print();
```

The -> operator is used with pointers to class objects.

```
String *sp = new String;
sp->print();
```

As with nonmember functions, there is compile time checking of member function calls. The type of the class object is used to identify the function and the actual arguments are matched to the parameter types in the function declaration.

Member functions operate on the class type object with which they are called. A pointer to this object is a hidden argument in all member functions and can be explicitly referred to in the function definition as `this`. No explicit use of `this` is needed in a member function. However, `this` is implicitly used for member references.

```
class String {
    char *str;
  public:
    void print() { printf( " %s", str ); }
};
```

In the above, the reference to the member `str` in `print` is the same as `this->str`. When `print` is called, `this` is set to the address of the object used in the call. For example `s.print()` sets `this` to `&s`, and therefore within `print`, the `str` referred to is `(&s)->str` or `s.str`. In the call `sp->print()`, `this` is set to `sp` and the member access is to `sp->str`.

All member functions are logically nested within the scope of their class. If a member function definition is given outside the body of a class definition, the scope of the function must be indicated by the scope operator with the class name.

```
class X {
    int f();
};

int X::f() { /* etc. */ }
```

The nesting of member functions within class scope makes the scoping rules different for member functions than for nonmember functions. In a member function, the declaration of an identifier is sought first at block scope, then at class scope, and finally at file scope. It is therefore possible for a member declaration to hide a file scope declaration. In the following example, the identifier x in function X::f() refers to the member, not the file scope variable x.

```
class X {
    int x;
    int f();
};

int x;

int X::f() { return x; }    // returns this->x
```

To reference the declaration of a file scope identifier hidden by a local or class scope declaration, the scope operator can be used. To change the above example so that X::f() returns the value of the file scope variable instead of the member, use :: to indicate the file scope x.

```
int X::f() { return ::x; }  // returns file scope x
```

The class scope is like a block around the member function. A declaration within a block scope of the function can hide the member declaration just as an inner block declaration can hide an outer block declaration. In the following case, X::f() returns the value of the local variable.

```
int X::f() { int x = 3; return x; }
```

Using the scope operator, the above can be changed to return either the member X::x, or file scope variable ::x.

3.4 Operator Functions

Language-defined operators can be overloaded to work on class type operands. This is done by providing an operator function that takes at least one class type argument. Operator function declarations and definitions are syntactically the same form as those of other functions, except the function name has the form operator *x* where *x* is the operator symbol being overloaded. The user-defined operators can be invoked with the usual infix expression syntax for the symbol *x*, as well as with a function call using the function name operator *x*. The operands of the expression serve as the arguments to the function call.

Because they are invoked with the same syntax, operator functions must have the same number of operands as the language-defined versions of the operators. Overloaded operators have the same precedence as the corresponding built-in operators.

Relationships among predefined operators, however, such as the equivalence of a+=b and a=a+b, or a[b] and *(a+b), or (&p)->x

and `p.x` , do not hold for user-defined operators unless the operator functions are implemented to make it so. The results of operator functions need not have any relation to the results of the predefined versions. In particular, user-defined ++ and −− cannot behave completely analogously to predefined versions. There is no way of defining different versions of these operators for their prefix and postfix forms, and so the same result is produced no matter which way these user-defined operators are used.

Suppose we add more operators to `class complex` from Chapter 1.

```
class complex {
    // etc.
    complex operator ++();
    complex operator +=( complex );
};
```

The single version of complex ++ will be used for both prefix and postfix forms, producing the same result for both.

```
complex c1, c2;
c2 = c1++;  // the same as c2 = ++c1;
```

The user-defined operator += may or may not be defined so that

```
c1 += c2;
```

is equivalent to

```
c1 = c1 + c2;
```

though it would probably be confusing if it weren't. Because `class complex` is intended to act as a numeric type, it is better to implement += to behave analogously to the built-in arithmetic operators.

Operator functions can be non-member or member functions, except for operators (), [] and −> which can only be member functions. If the operator function is a member, the implicit argument `this` is the first operand. In `class String` the `operator` <, which is implemented as a `friend`,

```
class String {
    char *str;
  public:
    friend int operator < ( String s1, String s2 )
        { return strcmp( s1.str, s2.str ) < 0; }
    // etc.
};
```

could also have been implemented as a member.

```
class String {
    char *str;
  public:
    int operator < ( String s2 )
        { return strcmp( str, s2.str ) < 0; }
    // etc.
};
```

If an operator function is a member, its first operand must always match the class type, without conversions being applied. Operator functions are often intended to behave analogously to their language-defined versions, in which conversions are applied to either operand. For this reason, operator functions are often implemented as `friend` functions.

Operator functions are functions with odd names, which work on class type arguments. They do not have to be called using infix notation, but can be called in the same way as any other function. For a nonmember function, all arguments are passed in the argument list.

```
class String {
    friend int operator < ( String, String );
    // etc.
};

void sort( String *a, int n ) {
    // etc.
            if( operator < ( a[i+1], a[i] ) {
                // etc.
```

For member functions, a member access operator is used.

```
class String {
    int operator < ( String );
    // etc.
};

void sort( String *a, int n ) {
    // etc.
            if( a[i+1].operator <( a[i] ) ) {
                // and so on
```

3.5 Access Protection and Friends

Class members can be either `public` (generally accessible) or `private` (access restricted to member and friend functions). The accessibility of members is indicated by their declaration in a section of the class definition headed by the label `public` or `private`. These labels can appear any number of times in a class definition and in any order. The first section of a class definition starts off as private until a label indicates a different protection level.

There is a third protection level in C++ that comes into play when class inheritance is used. A member can be specified as `protected`, in the same way that it can be specified `public` or `private`. When inheritance is not being used, protected members have the same access restrictions as private members. The use of protected members is discussed in Chapter 5.

Functions that have been declared `friend` in a class definition are not members of the class but have permission to access the private members of objects of the class type. One class can also be declared `friend` of another class, indicating that all member functions of the friend class are friends.

```
class Y;
class X {
    friend Y;
    int i;
    void f();
};

class Y {
    int f1( X& );
    void f2( X& );
    // etc.
};
```

In this example, the private members of X type objects, like the members `i` and `f()` of the `X&` arguments, can be accessed inside `Y::f1` and `Y::f2`. The member access operators must be used by friend functions because only members have `this`.

We have already noted that in a union, members are public unless otherwise indicated. *Structures* are another type of class, which are the same as classes except for the default member access level. In a structure definition, `struct` replaces `class` in the type definition. The first section of a structure starts off as public until a label indicates a different protection level.

```
struct String {
    String();
    String( char * );
    void print();
    friend int operator < ( String s1, String s2 );
    // etc.
  private:
    char *str;
};
```

In the above version of `String`, the member functions are all public, whereas the data member `str` is private.

3.6   Initialization and Conversions

If a class has constructors, a constructor always is used to initialize objects of the class type when they are created. In the string-sort example in this chapter, the constructor taking no arguments initializes the `String` array. For nonarray class objects, constructor arguments can be given to initialize objects at the point of declaration.

```
String s1( "hi" );

String s2 = "hi";
```

In the declarations above, both forms of initializers are used as constructor arguments to initialize the `String` objects `s1` and `s2`.

Constructor arguments can also be given when objects are created with operator `new`.

```
String *sp;

sp = new String( "hello" );
```

In the above, `sp` is set to point at a `String` that was initialized with a constructor using the argument `"hello"`. If arguments are not provided when a class object is declared or created, a constructor taking no arguments or having default arguments is used.

Class objects that are members of other class objects are also initialized with a constructor. Arguments for the constructor can be given in the member initialization list for the constructor of the enclosing class. Initializing values for any member, not only constructor arguments, can be specified in a constructor's member initialization list. Members that require initialization, like constant or reference type members, must have their initializers specified in the list. The member initialization list is separated by a colon from the constructor's argument list in the constructor's definition. It contains a list of member names, each of which is followed by a parenthesized list of constructor arguments or an initializing value.

```
enum { A, B, C };

class Node {
  public:
     int code;
     String str;

     Node( int, char * );
};

Node::Node( int c, char *s )
     : code( c ), str( s ) { }
```

The Node constructor in the above example initializes the member code with the value of the argument c, and passes its second argument s to the String constructor to initialize the Node member str. Given the above definition of Node, the code fragment

```
Node *np = new Node( A, "hello" );

np->str.print();
```

prints out

```
hello
```

It might seem that the use of the member initialization list could be replaced by assignments in the body of the constructor.

```
Node::Node( int c, char *s ) {
     code = c;
     str = s;
}
```

For the integer member code, there isn't much difference between the first assignment of a value in this new version of the Node constructor and the indication of an initializer in the initializer list. The member str is of String class type, however, which has constructors:

```
class String {
   char *str;
 public:
   String() { str = new char; *str = 0; }
   String( char *s ) {
      str = new char[ strlen(s)+1 ];
      strcpy( str, s );
   }
   // etc.
}
```

Whenever a `String` object is created, it is *always* initialized. Because no other initializer is specified, the default `String` constructor is used to initialize `str` when it is created. The assignment within the body of the `Node` constructor replaces the initial value of `str` with one that is the result of the conversion of the right-hand side of the assignment. There have been two calls to `String` constructors: one to initialize `str`, the second to convert s before the assignment. Assignment is not the same as initialization. Arguments for constructors that initialize members must be indicated in the member initializer list.

A constructor creates a class object value from its arguments and so converts the arguments to the class type. Constructors are not only initializers but conversion operators. This was shown in the string-sort program in which a pointer to an array of characters was converted to a `String` using a function-call style conversion and assigned to an element of a `String` array.

```
a[i] = String( buffer );
```

When a constructor takes one argument, it can also be invoked for conversion using the cast form of conversion operation

```
a[i] = ( String )buffer;
```

Function-call style or cast style conversions are generally interchangeable, although multiple-argument constructor conversions require the function-call style, and syntactically complex conversion type specifications require the cast style:

```
x = X(i,j);        // convert i and j to an X
fp = (int (*)())g; // convert g to a function pointer
```

Expression operands and function call arguments are automatically converted to the correct type if the needed language and/or user-defined conversion operations are available. At most one predefined conversion and one user-defined conversion will be applied automatically. It is an error if the choice of available conversions is ambiguous. An explicit conversion operation is necessary to force a conversion that cannot be done automatically.

Because conversions can be automatically applied, an explicit conversion operation is not needed to convert the `char *` input buffer to a `String` in the string-sort example. The availability of the `String( char * )` constructor provides a user-defined conversion from the right-hand-side to the left-hand-side type. An assignment that takes advantage of the automatically applied conversion

```
a[i] = buffer;
```

works just as well as the assignment with explicit conversion. In either case, the `String` constructor is used to convert the right-hand side.

Constructors provide conversions *to* the class type. It is also possible to provide conversions *from* the class type with conversion operator functions. These functions must be members of the class to be converted. They have names of the form `operator` *T* where *T* is a type name or specification of the type that is the conversion result.

We add to `class String` a conversion operator to convert a `String` back to a `char *`:

```
class String {
    char *str;
  public:
    operator char*();
    // etc.
};

String::operator char*() {
    char *p = new char[ strlen(str)+1 ];
    strcpy( p, str );
    return p;
}
```

Notice that `operator char*` makes a copy of the character array pointed to by `str` and returns a pointer to this new array. Simply returning the value of `str` provides the needed conversion, but this also gives away access to the data structure protected by `String`, leaving it open to possible misuse. Making a copy keeps the array pointed to by the member `str` accessible only through a `String` type object and the functions with `String` access privileges.

The following example demonstrates the use of the conversion operator and shows how the char * result can be used without affecting the original String. We have also slipped a new member into this example, ~String(). This is the *destructor* for class String. It is invoked whenever a String object goes out of scope. The destructor is used to deallocate the character array that was created by the String constructor. Notice that the default constructor has been changed. The delete operator deallocates storage allocated by new and should only be applied to objects created with new. Operator delete invokes the destructor for class objects before deallocating the object's storage.

```
#include <stdio.h>
#include <string.h>

class String {
    char *str;
  public:
    String() { str = new char; *str = 0; }
    String( char * );
    void print() { printf( " %s", str ); }
    operator char*();
    ~String() { delete str; }
    // etc.
};

String::String( char *s ) {
    str = new char[ strlen(s)+1 ];
    strcpy( str, s );
}

String::operator char*() {
    char *p = new char[ strlen(str)+1 ];
    strcpy( p, str );
    return p;
}
```

```
main() {
    String *sp = new String( "hello world?" );
    sp->print();

    char *cp;
    cp = ( char * )*sp;
    cp[11] = '!';
    printf( "\n %s \n", cp );

    sp->print();
    delete sp;

    cp[0] = 'H';
    cp[6] = 'W';
    printf( "\n %s \n", cp );
}
```

In this program, the explicit conversion of the `String` to `char  *`

```
    cp = ( char * )*sp;
```

was not needed because the conversion would have been done automatically. It was given only to mark the place of the use of `operator  char*`. The output of the program is

```
hello world?
hello world!
hello world?
Hello World!
```

3.7 Pointers to Class Members

Class members, other than `static` data members, are components of class objects. The addresses of class members are ''offsets'' relative to a particular object instance. The relative addresses of component class members are of type pointer to class member.

The type modifier for indicating a pointer to member in a declaration is $X::*$ where X is a class name. To dereference a pointer to member, operators `.*` and `->*`, are used. Like their related member access operators, the pointer to member dereference operators must be used with a class type left operand.

In the following small examples, we declare, set, and use pointers to members of a simple class.

```
class Node {
  public:
    int code;
    int num;
    void print();
    void report();
};
```

First the pointer to an `int` data member of `Node`:

```
int Node::*pi;

Node n, *np = new Node;
int i, j;

pi = &Node::code;
i = n.*pi;        // accesses n.code
j = np->*pi;      // accesses np->code

pi = &Node::num;
i = n.*pi;  // accesses n.num
j = np->*pi;      // accesses np->num
```

`pi` is declared to be a pointer to an `int` member of `Node`. It is set to point to `Node::code` and `Node::num` in turn and is used to access these members of `Node` type objects.

The type specification of a pointer to function member is somewhat complex, so we use a `typedef` to give the name `Pftype` to the type pointer to function member of `Node` taking no arguments and returning `void`. We then declare `pf` as a pointer of this type.

```
typedef void ( Node::*Pftype )();
Pftype pf;

pf = &Node::print;
(n.*pf)();   // calls n.print()
(np->*pf)();     // calls np->print()

pf = &Node::report;
(n.*pf)();   // calls n.report()
(np->*pf)();     // calls np->report()
```

The pointer `pf` is used to call first `Node::print`, and then `Node::report` for different `Node` objects. The parentheses are needed around the `n.*pf` and `np->*pf` to get the proper binding of the dereference operators over the call operator. Calling member functions in this way is the major use of pointers to members.

To demonstrate the use of a pointer to function member, we here extend
the string-sort function to put the list in an ascending or descending order,
depending on the value of an added third parameter. Member versions of
`String` comparison operators are used.

```
class String {
    // hidden implementation
  public:
    // etc.
    int operator < ( String s );
    int operator > ( String s );
};
```

The function `sort` declares a variable `compare` as a pointer to a member
function of `String`, taking a `String` argument and returning `int`. The
variable `compare` is a pointer to the type of the functions we want to
choose between, and it is set to either `String::operator > ` or
`String::operator <`.

```
void sort( String *a, int n, int descending ) {
    int changed;

    typedef int ( String::* Ftype ) ( String );
    Ftype compare = descending ?
            String::operator > :
                String::operator <;
    do {
        changed = 0;
        for( int i = 0; i < n-1; i++ )
            if( ( a[i+1].*compare )( a[i] ) ) {
                // exchange array elements
            }
    } while( changed );
}
```

The function call through the pointer,

```
    ( a[i+1].*compare )( a[i] )
```

is the same as either the infix operator function call

```
    a[i+1] > a[i]
```

or

```
    a[i+1] < a[i]
```

depending on the value of `compare`.

3.8 Exercises

Exercise 3-1. †Write a function that prints the bit representation of its `double` argument. □

Exercise 3-2. †Write a hash table class that stores and retrieves records with a character string key. Provide public member functions to insert, lookup, and remove records from the hash table. Hide the implementation details in the private part of the class. □

Exercise 3-3. Re-implement the hash table type of the previous exercise using a binary tree data structure without changing the declarations of the insert, lookup, and remove functions. Are we still justified in calling the result a hash table type? □

Exercise 3-4. †Show how a runtime trace of block entry and exit can be accomplished using constructors and destructors. □

CHAPTER 4: **Data Abstraction**

An abstract data type is an encapsulated data type that is accessible only through an interface that hides the implementation details of the type. The properties of an abstract data type are defined by its interface and not its internal structure, or implementation. The same abstract data type can therefore have different implementations at different times without affecting the code that uses it. It is in this sense that the data type is abstract: the properties of the type are defined by the interface, and the implementation details are abstracted away.

In C++, classes are used for data abstraction by hiding the implementation of a type in the private part of the class definition and providing an interface of publicly accessible operations. In this chapter we present several examples of abstract data types implemented with C++ classes and discuss issues of designing classes for data abstraction.

4.1 Complex Numbers

The complex number class presented in Chapter 1 is a good example of an abstract data type.

```
class complex {
    double re, im;
  public:
    friend complex operator +( complex, complex );
    // ...
    friend complex operator /( complex, complex );
    complex( double = 0.0, double = 0.0 );
};
```

Here we have decided to represent the complex number as its Cartesian coordinates in the complex plane. In the future, however, we may decide to change the implementation to use a polar representation. The representation used to implement complex numbers is hidden from general use in the private part of the class definition; therefore, we can make this change without affecting user code. The public interface defines the properties of the complex type. As long as this interface is maintained, user code is not affected by changes to the underlying implementation.

```
class complex {
    double theta;
    double r;
  public:
    friend
    complex operator *( complex a, complex b ) {
        complex result;
        result.r = a.r * b.r;
        result.theta = a.theta + b.theta;
        return result;
    }
    // ...
};
```

Because the abstract interface defines the semantics of the type for the user, an essential part of creating an abstract data type is the design of the interface. The design should reflect the abstract properties of the type, and not simply prevent users from changing the implementation. This is the difference between protection, described in Chapter 3, and data abstraction. An interface that protects the implementation of a type from unauthorized access without hiding its structure can still allow the code that uses it to develop dependencies on the implementation.

For example, if the interface for our complex type revealed the implementation to be a pair of doubles, users of complex could write code based on the assumption that a complex number was a Cartesian coordinate pair.

```
class complex {
    // ...
    double first() { return re; }
    double second() { return im; }
};
extern complex a;
complex b( a.first(), a.second() );
```

If complex is implemented as a coordinate pair, then a equals b. If we change the implementation to a polar representation, complex is still implemented as a pair of doubles, but a is no longer necessarily equal to b.

For complex numbers, the essential semantics of the type are embodied in a set of arithmetic operations and conversions from and to other numeric types.

Complex numbers can be added, subtracted, multiplied, and divided, so these properties are provided by overloading the operators +, −, *, and / to accept operands and produce results of type `complex`. It is not necessary to overload operators to provide this interface, as "regular" functions with appropriate access permission can also be used to implement the same abstract interface.

```
class complex {
    // ...
  public:
    friend complex add( complex, complex );
    // ...
    friend complex div( complex, complex );
    complex( double = 0, double = 0 );
};
```

The use of such functions for a complex number abstract data type, however, does not lead to a natural extension of the numeric types and operations already provided by the language. Compare

```
Z = add( add( R, mul( mul( j, omega ), L ) ),
         div( 1, mul( mul( j, omega ), C ) ) );
```

with the far more readable expression for AC impedance in Chapter 1.

```
Z = R + j * omega * L + 1/( j * omega * C );
```

Overloaded arithmetic operators provide an intuitive interface to class `complex`, but operator overloading can be abused. Because the semantics of the overloaded operator are determined by the implementer, it is possible to implement + to mean subtraction and − to mean addition, but in the absence of malicious intent it is unlikely that this will occur.

A more common abuse of operator overloading is overuse. For example, another property of complex numbers that should be represented in the abstract interface is exponentiation. Because C++ does not have an exponentiation operator it is tempting to press an existing operator into service, such as ^ (exclusive or), that does not have a useful meaning for complex numbers. Although this is possible, this particular use of operator overloading will introduce bugs and harm readability. The reason is that ^ has the wrong precedence for exponentiation. A user of class `complex` might code the expression $-1 + e^{i\pi}$ as `-1 + e^(i*pi)`, expecting the exponentiation operator to bind more tightly than addition, as it does in most languages that have a built-in exponentiation operator. Recall, however, that operator overloading does not change the existing precedences and associativities of operators, so the expression $-1 + e^\wedge(i*pi)$ is interpreted as $(-1 + e)^{i\pi}$, because $\wedge$ has lower precedence than +. It is better in this case to abandon operator overloading for the more pedestrian but clearer use of a nonoperator function.

```
-1 + pow( e, i*pi );
```

Operator overloading should be used only if the existing precedence and semantics of an operator support an intuitive understanding of its new use.

As we saw in Chapter 3, two kinds of functions have access to the private parts of a class definition: functions that are members of the class and functions that the class explicitly declares to be friends. Why did we choose to implement the arithmetic operations of complex numbers as friends rather than as members?

```
class complex {
    // ...
  public:
    // member operators
    complex operator +( complex );  // binary
    complex operator -( complex );  // binary
    complex operator -();    // unary
    // ...
};
```

The reason concerns the way in which complex numbers interact with other arithmetic types in mixed expressions.

The constructor for class complex (which, like the operator functions, is part of the abstract interface) has a dual role. In addition to ensuring that every object of type complex is initialized, it also specifies a conversion from a value of type double to one of type complex. There are predefined conversions from the other arithmetic types to double; thus, the constructor also specifies a conversion to complex from the other predefined arithmetic types. The constructor is invoked as necessary to provide this conversion on assignment or initialization of a complex by a predefined arithmetic type.

```
complex x = 12.34;  // complex( 12.34, 0 )
x = 12;     // complex( (double)12, 0 )
```

The constructor is therefore invoked as necessary to perform conversions for the initialization of function formal arguments with the actual arguments of the call.

```
complex add( complex, complex );
complex a, b;
double c, d;
// ...
add( a, b );
add( a, d );    // add( a, complex(d) );
add( c, b );    // add( complex(c), b );
```

An operator function is not essentially different from a nonoperator function, and may be called either as an infix operator or as a nonoperator function.

```
complex operator +( complex, complex );
a + b;
operator +( a, b ); // same as above
a + d;
operator +( a, d ); // ditto here,
c+b;
operator +( c, b ); // and here.
```

Consider trying to write the same sequence of expressions using a member operator function.

```
a + b;
a.operator +( b );   // fine...
a + d;
a.operator +( d );   // fine...
c + b;               // error!
c.operator +( b );   // error!
```

The trouble with the addition of c and b above is that we are attempting to call an operator function that is a member of c, but c isn't of class type and has no members! Whether it's written as c+b or as c.operator +(b), the expression makes no sense. If we had implemented the complex operator functions as members, the users of our type could never write an expression in which the first operand of a complex operator was a noncomplex number without supplying an explicit conversion.

The implementation of operations on complex numbers by overloading the existing operators and by supplying initialization and conversion semantics with a constructor allows us to extend the arithmetic type system of C++ to include complex numbers that can be used as easily and as naturally as the built-in arithmetic types.

4.2   Strings

As a further example of data abstraction, let's look at a modified version
of the String data type of Chapter 3.

```
class String_rep {
    char *str;
    int refs;
    String_rep( char * );
    friend class String;
};


class String {
    String_rep *r;
  public:
    friend String operator +( String, String );
    friend int operator <( String, String );
    // other operators...
    String &operator =( String );
    operator char *();
    String( char * = "" );
    String( String & );
    ~String();
};
```

In this version of the String class we've decided to share the actual character strings as much as possible, and have created a class, String_rep,
that binds together a character string and a reference count. The String
class now refers to this data structure instead of referring directly to the
character string.

The first constructor is very simple, specifying how to initialize a
String with a character string (and, as with the constructor for class
complex, specifying a conversion from a character string to a String).

```
String::String( char *s ) {
    r = new String_rep( s );
}
```

Class String_rep takes care of its own initialization.

```
String_rep::String_rep( char *s ) {
    str = new char[ strlen(s)+1 ];
    strcpy( str, s );
    refs = 1;
}
```

When one String is initialized with another, instead of creating a
second copy of the character string, we refer to the existing representation

and increment its reference count. We specify these semantics with a constructor that takes a `String&` argument.

```
String::String( String &init ) {
    r = init.r;
    r->refs++;
}
```

The semantics of assignment are similar, but we must also be concerned
about the `String_rep` to which the left operand (the target) of the assignment referred before being assigned its new value. The reference count of
the `String_rep` is decremented because the `String` being assigned will
no longer refer to it. If there are no references remaining, the
`String_rep` is deleted.

```
String &
String::operator =( String str ) {
    if( !--r->refs )
        delete r;
    r = str.r;
    r->refs++;
    return *this;
}
```

To parallel the behavior of the built-in assignment operator, the assignment operator for `String` not only changes the object being assigned to
but also returns the value of the object. The `this` pointer is used to access
the object in order to return its value.

Note the difference in semantics of assignment and initialization between
`Strings` and complex numbers. In the case of our implementation of
complex numbers, the predefined semantics of assignment and initialization
are sufficient, and the representation of one complex number is simply
copied member by member into another. In order to have a correct implementation of `Strings`, the reference count in the `String_rep` to which
the `String` refers must be updated on assignment. It is therefore necessary to provide `operator =` for class `String`.

In general, if it is necessary to supply assignment for an abstract data
type, it is a good idea to also supply initialization and vice versa. In the
`String` type, supplying one without the other would cause as much trouble as their omission altogether. Together, these operations specify how objects of a given class type are to be copied in all situations. We will have
more to say about copy semantics in Chapter 7.

We must also take care to adjust reference counts for `Strings` that are
deleted or that go out of scope. For this we define a destructor.

```
String::~String() {
    if( !--r->refs )
        delete r;
}
```

As in the complex number type, we've supplied overloaded operators and a constructor in order to interface well with the existing type system of C++. One of the constructors supplies a conversion from character strings to `Strings`, and the concatenation operation is supplied by overloading operator + as a friend, as the complex arithmetic operators are.

```
extern char *home_dir, *path, *file;
String home = home_dir;
String fpath = home + "/" + path + "/" + file;
```

To complete the interface of the `String` type with the existing type system, we supply an operator that defines a conversion from a `String` to a `char *`. In this version of the conversion operator, unlike the one of Chapter 3, we take the more efficient but potentially more dangerous approach of returning the address of the character string rather than the address of a copy of the string.

```
String::operator char *() {
    return r->str;
}
// ...
char *newfile = fpath;   // fpath.operator char *()
```

This conversion in effect supplies the inverse function of a constructor. The `String` class's constructors specify how to create a `String` from a `char *` or another `String`, whereas the conversion operator `operator char *` specifies how to create a `char *` from a `String`. This capability is important for completing the interface to the existing C++ type system in that it provides for an interface to existing code written for objects of type `char *`.

```
extern FILE *fopen( const char *, const char * );
FILE *fp = fopen( fpath, "r+" );
```

As with a constructor, the conversion operator is invoked as required in expressions and initializers.

Unlike the overloaded + operator for concatenation, and unlike the complex arithmetic operators, we have implemented `String` assignment as a member function. The reason is that the ''handedness'' engendered by members with respect to automatic argument conversion is precisely what is

required for assignment; we do not want conversions applied to the left argument of an assignment.

If `operator` `=` were implemented as a friend function, it would then
be possible to assign `String`s to character strings, because the `char` `*` on
the left side of the assignment would be automatically converted to a
`String` by the `String` constructor that takes a `char` `*` argument.

```
"/usr/bin" = pathname;
```

Recall that the use of overloaded infix operators is just a notational convenience and is entirely equivalent to a function call.

```
operator =( "/usr/bin", pathname );
```

Therefore, although we probably don't want to allow assignments to character strings like `"/usr/bin"` this is nevertheless correct if `operator=` is
not a member of class `String`. In making = a member function, the assignment above makes as much sense as

```
"/usr/bin".operator =( pathname );
```

that is, it makes no sense at all. Implementing `String` assignment as a
member function prevents such conversions from being applied to the left
operand of the assignment. The more reasonable semantics of assigning or
initializing a `char` `*` with a `String` is already handled by the conversion
operator.

The proper use of operator functions, constructors, and conversion operators allows us to design abstract data types that merge with and extend the
predefined type system of C++.

4.3 Sorted Collections

Data abstraction confers two major, and equally important, advantages
on its users. First, it simplifies the semantics of using a type to what is explicitly represented in the public interface. Users of the type don't have to
contend with implementation-dependent semantics that have no meaning for
the abstract function of the type. For example, users of the `String` type
don't have to worry about maintaining reference counts when doing assignments or overflowing buffers when doing concatenations. These "secondary" semantics are the property of the hidden implementation and are the
responsibility of the implementer of the type. By the same token, the implementer is free to change the implementation without fear of affecting the
meaning of user code so long as the semantics are preserved.

Equally important is the ability of data abstraction to bring the programming language closer to a specific problem domain. The ability to define `complex` and `String` data types gives users of those types the ability to write compact, clear programs involving complex arithmetic and string manipulation because, in effect, the C++ language has been extended to aid the developer to both *think* and *code* in these problem areas. This use of data abstraction as support for conceptual abstraction in program design is most important.

Complex numbers and strings are data types with a wide range of applicability, and in fact are built-in types in many programming languages. Well-designed abstract data types, however, can confer similar advantages for more specialized application areas as well.

For instance, some applications may have need for a type that represents the semantics of a sorted collection of integers. Using the same techniques we did for `complex` and `String` we define the public interface for such a type.

```
typedef int ETYPE;

class sorted_collection {
  public:
    sorted_collection();
    void insert( ETYPE );
    void apply( void (*)(ETYPE) );
};
```

This class represents a simple concept and therefore has a simple interface: there are operations to create a `sorted_collection`, insert a new integer into the collection, and apply a function to each element of the collection in sorted sequence.

Now that the interface is defined, users of the type can start to design and code applications.

```
#include "collection.h"

printint() {
    // read in, sort and print some integers
    extern void print( int );
    extern int read( int & );
    sorted_collection sc;
    int i;
    while( read( i ) )
        sc.insert( i );
    sc.apply( print );
}
```

While users work with the interface to `sorted_collection`, we can complete a first implementation of it.

```
typedef int ETYPE;

class sorted_collection {
    ETYPE ary[ 100 ];
    int free;
  public:
    sorted_collection() { free = 0; }
    void insert( ETYPE );
    void apply( void (*)(ETYPE) );
};

void
sorted_collection::apply( void (*f)(ETYPE) ) {
    for( int i = 0; i != free; i++ )
        f( ary[ i ] );
}


void
sorted_collection::insert( ETYPE el ) {
    for( int i = free++; i && ary[ i-1 ] > el; i-- )
        ary[ i ] = ary[ i-1 ];
    ary[ i ] = el;
}
```

This implementation is clearly not very good. The insertion algorithm is inefficient for large collections. This inefficiency, however, is unlikely to cause problems because, long before it is noticeable, a large collection of integers will overrun the fixed-size collection array and bomb the program. The only positive point one can make about the implementation is that it took only a few minutes to write. This is advantage enough, because now users of the type can compile and begin to debug their applications while we work on providing a better implementation. Quick implementations like this are also useful in the initial design stages of a programming project, when the public interface to an abstract data type has not yet been fixed. In this way, users can experiment with the type and modify its interface without causing any expensively produced code to be invalidated.

We now refine our implementation.

```
typedef int ETYPE;

class tree {
    ETYPE el;
    tree *lchild, *rchild;
    tree( ETYPE i ) { el = i; lchild = rchild = 0; }
    void insert( ETYPE );
    void apply( void (*)(ETYPE) );
    friend sorted_collection;
};

void
tree::insert( ETYPE i ) {
    if( i < el )
        if( lchild )
            lchild->insert( i );
        else
            lchild = new tree( i );
    else
        if( rchild )
            rchild->insert( i );
        else
            rchild = new tree( i );
}

void
tree::apply( void (*f)(ETYPE) ) {
    if( lchild )
        lchild->apply( f );
    f( el );
    if( rchild )
        rchild->apply( f );
}
```

```
    class sorted_collection {
        tree *root;
      public:
        sorted_collection() { root = 0; }
        void insert( ETYPE el ) {
            if( root )
                root->insert( el );
            else
                root = new tree( el );
        }
        void apply( void (*f)(ETYPE) )
            { if( root ) root->apply( f ); }
    };
```

Our second implementation is better than the first in that it can handle large collections, and element insertion is much more efficient. Unless they run up against one of the limitations of the first implementation (and bomb), however, users of the type cannot distinguish between implementations. Each implementation is just a different representation of the same abstract type, and the abstract semantics are unchanged from one implementation to the other.

This is not to say that these "secondary," or implementation-specific, semantics cannot have a profound effect on the behavior of programs that use the type. Our initial implementation of sorted_collection has the implicit assumption that no user program will attempt to insert more than 100 integers in a given collection. Because this limitation is not represented in the abstract interface, however, users of the type are not aware of it and may violate the restriction.

More insidious are situations in which programs take advantage of implementation-specific semantics that are not explicitly part of the abstract semantics of a type. For example, we can create a collection data type (whose elements do not *have* to be sorted) from a sorted collection.

```
    typedef sorted_collection collection;
```

Unfortunately a user of this type can write a program that takes advantage of the fact that the collection just happens to be sorted. Later we may reimplement collection to do more efficient insertions than sorted_collection by not sorting, effectively invalidating programs that depend on the implementation-specific semantics.

For these reasons it is often useful to view the public interface to an abstract data type as a contract between implementer and user of the type. The implementer is required to supply the correct abstract semantics specified by the interface without making any unnecessary additional assumptions, and users of the type should assume only those semantics explicitly present in the public interface.

4.4 Genericity

A sorted collection of integers is a useful data type for certain applications, but so are sorted collections of `doubles`, `Strings`, and even sorted collections. It is clear that the abstraction with which we are concerned is a sorted collection in general, and not a sorted collection of objects of any one type. What we would like to be able to do is parameterize our implementation of `sorted_collection` and then instantiate, or create, instances of it for specific element types. In this way, a single parameterized implementation of `sorted_collection` can serve as a generic representation of the semantics of sorted collections. Each instantiation will produce a new sorted collection type for a specified element type. Users would then be able to declare and use objects of these instantiated types.

Unfortunately, the C++ language does not currently support the concept of generic, or parameterized, types. It is possible, however, to achieve much of the capability of parameterized types using other features of the language.

Consider our second implementation of `sorted_collection`. We have actually implemented the type to work with elements of type `ETYPE`, where `ETYPE` has been defined with a `typedef` to be an `int`. What properties of `ETYPE` are used by our implementation? Looking through the code, we find that an `ETYPE` must have the operators = and < defined for it, and it must be possible to initialize one `ETYPE` with another (in order to initialize the `ETYPE` formal argument of the function pointer in `sorted_collection::apply`). Simply changing the `typedef` to define `ETYPE` as some other type with these properties will, in effect, instantiate a version of `sorted_collection` for the given `ETYPE`.

```
typedef String ETYPE;
class sorted_collection {
    // ...
};
printString() {
    // sort and print the input sentences,
    // removing objectionable text
    extern void print( char * );
    extern void censor( char * );
    extern char *readstr();
    sorted_collection list;
    char *s;
    while( s = readstr() )
        list.insert( s );
    list.apply( censor );
    list.apply( print );
}
```

(Note how the implicit conversions described earlier in this chapter from String to char * and vice versa are employed above.)

This scheme works well if we need no more than one sorted collection type in each file but cannot be used for multiple instantiations. An ETYPE cannot be two types simultaneously! The only recourse is to copy the implementation of sorted_collection and edit each copy to produce multiple versions of the implementation for different element types. Typically, the preprocessor is used to do the editing.

One of the standard C++ header files, generic.h, contains preprocessor macro definitions to aid with these editing operations. Macros are provided to concatenate names, and to declare and define generic types.

One problem in defining multiple instantiations of a generic type from a single template is in creating a unique name for each instantiated type. We use the name2 macro from generic.h to help with this task.

```
#define sorted_collection(ETYPE) \
        name2(ETYPE,sorted_collection)
#define tree(ETYPE) name2(ETYPE,tree)
```

Here we create unique names for our class types by concatenating the type parameter with the generic type names. For example, the text tree(String) will be converted by the tree macro to Stringtree. The implementation of the name2 macro is simple but can vary from preprocessor to preprocessor. For an ANSI C preprocessor, name2 would be implemented with the concatenation operator.

```
#define name2(a,b) a##b
```

To instantiate a new version of a generic type, `generic.h` provides the `declare` macro.

```
#define declare(a,t) name2(a,declare)(t)
```

A user creating a "sorted collection of `String`s" type would use it as follows:

```
declare(sorted_collection,String);
```

After expansion, this would produce

```
sorted_collectiondeclare(String);
```

`sorted_collectiondeclare` is yet another macro. As providers of the generic `sorted_collection` type, we must define this macro.

```
#define sorted_collectiondeclare(ETYPE) \
class tree(ETYPE) { \
    ETYPE el; \
    tree(ETYPE) *l, *r; \
    tree(ETYPE)( ETYPE i ) { el = i; l = r = 0; } \
    void insert( ETYPE ); \
    void apply( void (*)(ETYPE) ); \
    friend sorted_collection(ETYPE); \
}; \
class sorted_collection(ETYPE) { \
    tree(ETYPE) *root; \
    public: \
    sorted_collection(ETYPE)() { root = 0; } \
    void insert( ETYPE el ) \
        { if( root ) root->insert( el ); }\
    void apply( void (*f)(ETYPE) )   \
        { root->apply( f ); } \
};
```

When the `sorted_collectiondeclare` macro is expanded with its type argument, the argument is substituted for `ETYPE`, and the macros we defined earlier, `sorted_collection` and `tree`, are invoked as necessary to create the unique class names for the generic `tree` and `sorted_collection` classes.

Users can now instantiate versions of our generic sorted collection class and declare objects of the instantiated types.

```
#include <generic.h>
#include "collection.h"
#include "String.h"

declare(sorted_collection,int);
declare(sorted_collection,String);

printint() {
    // ...
    sorted_collection(int) sc;
    int i;
    while( read( i ) )
        sc.insert( i );
    sc.apply( print );
}


printString() {
    // ...
    sorted_collection(String) list;
    char *s;
    while( s = readstr() )
        list.insert( s );
    list.apply( censor );
    list.apply( print );
}
```

In addition to the class definitions for each instantiated version of
sorted_collection, generated once for each file in which they are
used, corresponding definitions of the member functions tree::insert
and tree::apply must be generated exactly once in the entire program
for each instantiated type. To do this, we proceed exactly as we did for the
class definitions but make sure that we define these functions only once in
the program for each type parameter. To help distinguish these parallel
operations, generic.h provides a macro, implement, that is identical in
function to declare.

By proceeding in a manner analogous to the above, it is possible to define and use generic types that require more than a single type parameter for
instantiation. Note that generic.h provides name3, declare2, and so
forth, macros for developing and using such types.

4.5   Control Abstraction

The `apply` function of class `sorted_collection` is really a composition of two separate concepts: traversal of whatever data structure is used to hold the elements of a `sorted_collection` and applying a function to an element of the collection. Both of these concepts, as well as their composition as in the `apply` function, belong to a general class of abstractions that we call control abstractions.

Traversal of the hidden representation of a data structure without any attendant operation is clearly of little use. If the traversal can be broken up into stages, however, each of which yields some interesting value, then users of the type can access values associated with the type in a way that preserves the privacy of the hidden implementation. A control abstraction of this kind is called an *iterator*.

Consider the implementation of a list type. A list has a head, a tail, and a sequence of elements in between. We would like to design a mechanism that gives access to the values of the list elements in sequence.

```
struct node {
    node *next;
    ETYPE el;
    node( ETYPE i, node *n ) { el = i; next = n; }
};

class list {
    node *hd;
  public:
    list( node *n = 0 ) { hd = n; }
    list( list &seq ) { hd = seq.hd; }
    void insert( ETYPE i )
        { hd = new node( i, hd ); }
    friend ETYPE head( list seq )
       { return seq.hd->el; }
    friend list tail( list seq )
        { return list( seq.hd->next ); }
    friend int isempty( list seq )
        { return seq.hd == 0; }
};
```

```
void
print_list( list seq ) {
    extern void print( ETYPE );
    for( list s = seq; !isempty(s); s = tail(s) )
        print( head( s ) );
}
```

This is a useful abstraction if one has the habit of thinking of lists recursively; that is, a list is empty, or it is a list element followed by a list. In this case we want to think about lists iteratively, however, as a sequence of list elements and not as a recursively defined sequence of lists. Although the above abstraction is effective, in that it allows us to access the elements of the list in sequence, it doesn't support our way of thinking, so we try a second version:

```
class list {
    ETYPE el;
    list *link;
  public:
    list( ETYPE i, list *next )
        { el = i; link = next; }
    list *next() { return link; }
    ETYPE value() { return el; }
};


void
print_list( list *seq ) {
    extern void print( ETYPE );
    for( list *p = seq; p; p = p->next() )
        print( p->value() );
}
```

The view of this second implementation is certainly iterative in nature, but we have somehow lost our list abstraction altogether and are left only with list elements.

Here's another version:

```
class node {
    node *next;
    ETYPE el;
    node( ETYPE, node * );
    friend list;
    friend iter;
};
```

```
class list {
    node *hd;
  public:
    list();
    void insert( ETYPE );
    friend iter;
};

class iter {
    node *current;
  public:
    iter(list);
    ETYPE *operator()();
};


void
print_list( list lst ) {
    extern void print( ETYPE );
    iter next = lst;
    ETYPE *p;
    while( p = next() )
        print( *p );
}
```

Here we have designed an iterator type, associated with the list type, that embodies the control abstraction of sequencing through the elements of type list in the same way that the list type embodies the abstraction of the list data structure. To iterate through the elements of a list, we create an iteration object and bind it to a list object on initialization.

```
iter::iter( list ilist ) {
    current = ilist.hd;
}
```

The iterator object itself retains the state of the iteration from invocation to invocation.

```
ETYPE *
iter::operator()() {
    if( current ) {
        node *tmp = current;
        current = current->next;
        return &tmp->el;
    }
    return 0;
}
```

This iterator has only a single operation; it gets the next list element. In this case we have decided to use the overloaded () operator to express this operation, but we could have just as well overloaded ++ or used a nonoperator member function, or even a nonmember friend.

```
class iter {
    // ...
  public:
    // ...
    ETYPE *operator () ();    // next()
    ETYPE *operator ++();     // next++ or ++next
    ETYPE *next();            // next.next()
    friend ETYPE *nxt( iter );  // nxt( next )
};
```

The essential idea is that the iterator object has a concept of the state of the iteration that it retains from invocation to invocation.

This view of a list is what we are after. We have retained the concept of a list as an entity in itself, but have the capability of sequencing through its elements in a natural way. The iterator is, in effect, an extension of the list class that provides an abstract flow-of-control operation. This creation of abstract flow-of-control types that are applied in conjunction with abstract data types is a powerful mechanism for working with abstract types with complex internal structure in an implementation-independent manner.

The iterator for our list class is very simple; with each invocation, it gets the next element of the list until there are no more elements. We could have implemented more complex semantics, however. For instance, creation of an iterator for a list could have the side effect of locking the list so no new elements can be inserted until the iteration is complete. We could have defined more general motion on lists. For instance, we could add a scanning function to class `iter` that returns the next list element that satisfies an argument predicate function,

```
class employee {
    // ...
  public:
    int ismgr();
    int istrue() { return 1; }
};

typedef employee ETYPE;
```

```
class list {
    // ...
};

class iter {
    // ...
  public:
    ETYPE *operator () ();
    ETYPE *operator () ( int (ETYPE::*) () );
};


void
clean_up( list alist, int all ) {
    extern void print( employee );
    extern void fire( employee );
    iter next = alist;
    employee *e;
    while( e = next() )
        print( *e );
    int (employee::*predicate) ()
        = all ? employee::istrue : employee::ismgr;
    iter next_victim = alist;
    while( e = next_victim( predicate ) )
        fire( *e );
}
```

or we could add the ability to back up to the previous element or to the head of the list. Note also that an iterator object can be assigned to another iterator object or passed as an argument to a function, and that there can be multiple concurrently active iterator objects for the same list.

Multiple iterator types (as well as multiple objects of the same iterator type) can be created for the same abstract type. A tree data type might define various iterators for preorder, postorder, breadth first, and depth first traversals.

The two central ideas behind control abstraction are the same as those we discussed earlier in this chapter for data abstraction in general. First, the user of a control abstraction is unaffected by the details of its implementation. In addition to reducing the amount of knowledge that must be acquired before a user can write a simple flow-of-control structure, the implementer of a type can change its implementation (and the implementation of the type's associated control abstractions) without affecting user code.

Second, control abstraction brings the programming language closer to the control aspects of the problem in the same way that data abstraction does for the type aspects. This is especially valuable in more complex situations, in which the concept of what is going on would otherwise be lost in the details of its implementation.

Some techniques are so obvious that they can be overlooked, like the capability of providing read-only class members. In some situations an implementer may want to provide a window into a private part of a type's implementation, or, equivalently, the implementer may want users of a type to examine part of the public interface without changing it. This capability can be provided with inline functions.

```
class node {
    node *n;
    ETYPE val;
  public:
    // ...
    node *next() { return n; }
    ETYPE value() { return val; }
};
// ...
for( node *p = head; p; p - p->next() )
    print( p->value() );
```

In this case, the implementation *is* the abstraction, but we don't want users of the node type to change the list structure or element values.

Another simple control technique is provided by applicators. An applicator is a function that applies one of its arguments to the others.

```
void apply( char *s, void(*f)( char * ) ) {
    f( s );
}
```

This is a simple applicator that applies its function (pointer) argument to its character string argument.

```
String pathname = "/usr/cmd";
extern void exec( char * );
extern char *cmd;
apply( pathname + "/" + cmd, exec );
```

Clearly we could have implemented this more effectively by calling the function directly, so of what use are applicators? We've already seen the use of an applicator in our `sorted_collection` class, albeit in alloyed form. The member `apply` function is the composition of a traversal and an applicator that allows users of `sorted_collection` to apply a function to each member of the collection. We describe additional uses of applicators in Chapter 8.

It is clear at this point that there is no obvious dividing line between control and data abstraction, or between abstract and nonabstract data types, nor should there be. The data abstraction paradigm is not a rigid formalism that spells out "how software should be written." Rather, it is an opportunity to unleash your imagination in deciding what data types your problem deals with. Integers, complex numbers, strings, lists, communication networks, telephones, and grammars all have (at least as far as programs are concerned) abstract properties that can be represented in the public interface to an abstract data type. Data abstraction is also an invitation to create new implementations of these types and new control structures to make working with them natural.

4.6 Exercises

Exercise 4-1. Change the implementation of class `complex` to use polar coordinates instead of (real, imaginary) pairs. How does this change affect user code? □

Exercise 4-2. Design a complex type similar to class `complex` that uses `floats` instead of `doubles` for the representation. Make this work seamlessly with the existing class `complex` and the predefined arithmetic types, so that short complex numbers can be used in mixed expressions with complex numbers and other arithmetic types. Can you make the polar representation in the previous exercise work with the nonpolar representations? □

Exercise 4-3. Use genericity to implement both regular and short complex numbers from a common generic class. □

Exercise 4-4. Consider a date abstract data type with the following interface:

```
class Date {
  public:
    const char *str();
    Date( char * );
    Date( int, int, int );
    Date &operator ++();
    Date &operator --();
};
```

A `Date` is initialized either with a character string representation of a date such as 17 June 1775 or by three integers representing day, month, and year: 17, 6, 1775. The conversion operator returns a pointer to a character string representation of the date. The ++ and -- operators increment and decrement the date by one day, respectively.

Provide three different implementations of this abstract data type, using a single integer, three integers, and a character string to implement the internal form of a date. What are the relative merits of each implementation? What are the merits of having a single abstract type for all three implementations? □

Exercise 4-5. Most calculations relating to physical systems are not composed solely of scalar operands but also contain operands with associated physical units. For example, the calculation of AC inductance involves calculation with elements in ohms, farads, and so forth. It is a useful check when doing such calculations to carry the algebraic operations through on the physical unit types as well as on the numeric values of the operands. The calculated physical unit type should match the expected result type. Design integer, floating point, and complex data types that include associated physical units. Overload the arithmetic operators to calculate both the correct arithmetic and physical unit of the result. Provide conversions between the types and the predefined and complex arithmetic types. □

Exercise 4-6. Design a directed graph data type and consider the following points: Is the representation hidden? Is the interface as small and clean as possible? On the other hand, is the interface rich enough to allow users of the type to write useful procedures? □

Exercise 4-7. Write an iterator for the graph abstract data type above that follows the sequence of nodes for a set of depth first spanning trees for the graph. (Hint: Pay careful attention to how you record the state of the iteration. Will you be able to iterate through very large graphs?) □

Exercise 4-8. Design a finite state automaton data type. What is the set of initializers for this type (a function pointer for a function that returns a description, an input description file?). What error conditions should be detected when constructing the type? What are the uses of such a type? Can a single representation serve for both the directed graph abstraction and the FSA? Why or why not, and what are the relative advantages of having a single representation or two representations? □

Exercise 4-9. Think of a useful data type that is not represented as a built-in type for any programming language, and implement the type as an abstract data type in C++. Write a program using this data type. □

Exercise 4-10. Suppose you were designing a portable compiler. How would you separate the common parts of the compiler from the machine-dependent parts? Could you represent the interface to these machine-dependent parts of the compilation process as an abstract data type? □

Exercise 4-11. C++ does not automatically check at runtime to see if array accesses are within bounds. Design a generic array type that does bounds checking. □

Exercise 4-12. Rewrite the `String` type to dispense with reference counting, taking care not to change the abstract interface. Is the constructor `String(String&)` still necessary? How about `operator =`? □

Exercise 4-13. Design a histogram data type by overloading `operator[]` to index with floating arguments. □

Exercise 4-14. †Design an associative array type for a dictionary (mapping `String=>String`). Make the type generic by supplying type parameters for both index and element type of the array. Instantiate a version of the type that indexes a dictionary with a `String`. What other useful types might be instantiated from this generic associative array type? □

Exercise 4-15. Implement a general list iterator that has operations to return the next element, the previous element, and the head of the list. Implement this iterator without changing the implementation of the `list` class. □

Exercise 4-16. †Design a two-way list whose implementation uses only a single link pointer. Include in your design an iterator that can traverse the list in either direction. □

CHAPTER 5: **Inheritance**

Data abstraction is an effective technique for extending the predefined type system when one can define a single, clearly defined concept, like the `complex`, `String`, and `sorted_collection` types of the previous chapter. We may sometimes have an abstract data type, however, that is *almost*, but not quite, what we want, or a collection of types that are similar in implementation or meaning without being identical. In these cases inheritance is a useful technique for augmenting data abstraction.

Inheritance in C++ is a mechanism for building class types from other class types, defining a new class type to be a specialization or augmentation of an existing class type. This chapter covers the mechanics and use of inheritance for coding, design, and abstraction.

5.1 Base and Derived Classes

A class can inherit the features or functionality of another class through class derivation. The class derived from the original, or base, class can add to or tailor the features of the base class to produce either a specialization or augmentation of the base class type, or simply to reuse the implementation of the base class.

For instance, we can think of a doubly linked list as a singly linked list with an extra link and an additional operation to access the previous element, as well as the next. We start with the list node class of the previous chapter.

```
class list {
    ETYPE el;
    list *link;
  public:
    list( ETYPE, list * );
    list *next();
    ETYPE value();
};
```

We then use class derivation to define a doubly linked list node class using class list as a starting point.

```
class list2 : public list {
    list2 *link;
  public:
    list2( ETYPE, list2 *, list2 * );
    list2 *previous();
};
```

The syntax

```
class list2 : public list
```

declares list2 to be a new class derived from class list. We also say that list is a base class of list2. list2 inherits all of list's members, both data and function, and adds its own: a link to the previous list node, a function for accessing that link, and a constructor.

The implementation of the member function previous is similar to that of next in class list.

```
list2 *
list2::previous() {
    return link;
}
```

Class list2 has two different members named link: the original forward link inherited from its base class, and the backward link declared within the body of list2. The link returned by previous is that of list2, in consequence of how class scope is affected by derivation.

Class derivation builds a hierarchy of nested class scopes. The scope of a derived class nests within the scope of its base class, in much the same way that an inner block of a function nests within an enclosing block. Therefore, when we refer to link in a member function of list2, the compiler will first look for link in the scope of class list2, and only check the base class scope if the name is not found. In cases in which one wants to access a base class member hidden by a derived class member with the same spelling, the syntax base::member can be used to specify that name lookup start in the scope of `base`.

The function `whatsbefore` accesses both inherited and regular members in the same way.

```
list2 *
whatsbefore( list2 *lst, ETYPE e ) {
    for( list2 *p = lst; p; p = (list2 *)p->next() )
        if( p->value() == e )
            break;
    if( p )
        return p->previous();
    else
        return 0;
}
```

Nested class scope explains why this code works. Only the call to `previous` refers to a member explicitly declared in `list2`. The calls to `next` and `value` refer to inherited base class member functions.

Alternatively, we could have supplied `list2` with a full complement of member functions for list traversal and access to the element value.

```
class list2 : public list {
    list2 *link;
  public:
    list *next();
    list2 *previous();
    ETYPE value();
};
```

We soon run into problems, however. Consider the implementation of `list2::next`.

```
list *
list2::next() {
    return list::link;   // error!
}
```

Here we attempt to return the value of the forward link from the base class. This is an error, however, because `list::link` is private. Unless it's declared to be a friend, a derived class does not have any special access privileges to its base class's private members. Our only choice is to use `list`'s public interface to access the value

```
return list::next();
```

which will work but hardly seems worth the effort when the same behavior is obtained by doing nothing at all.

Recall that the class definition for `list2` started with

```
class list2 : public list
```

The keyword `public` in this context specifies that the public members of `list` will also be public to users of `list2`. If the keyword `private` were used, or if neither `public` nor `private` were used, then the public members of `list` would be private when accessed through `list2`. For example, in function `whatsbefore` all references to `value` and `next` would be erroneous references to private members. Note that the members and friends of `list2` have access to the public members of `list` whether or not it is a public or private base class.

Finer granularity of access to public base class data members can be achieved with public base member declarations in a derived class. A public base member declaration has the form

```
Base::member;
```

where `Base` is the name of a base class, and `member` is a public member of that base class. The declaration must occur in a public part of the derived class definition.

```
class otherlist {
  public:
    otherlist *forw;
    ETYPE el;
};
```

```
class otherlist2 : private otherlist {
  public:
    otherlist::forw;
    otherlist2 *back;
};
```

Although `otherlist` is a private base class of `otherlist2`, the public base class declaration of `forw` allows it to be accessed as a public member through `otherlist2`. Because `otherlist::el` is not declared as a public base member, it is private when accessed through `otherlist2`.

Derived class constructors can include explicit initialization of a base class in the member initialization list. The constructor for `list2` uses a member initialization list to initialize its base class, just as it would initialize a member. The initialization of a base class is entirely analogous to initialization of class members described in Chapter 3, except that a base class is always (explicitly or implicitly) initialized before any member, even if a member initializer appears before the base class initializer on the member

initialization list. If a base class has no constructor, it need not be initialized, and if it has a constructor that can be invoked without arguments, it
need not be explicitly initialized.

```
list2::list2( ETYPE e, list2 *fl, list2 *bl )
                 : list( e, fl ) {
     link = bl;
}
```

Just as with a member initialization, a base class initialization may be
any legal initializer for an object of the base class type, and not just a constructor initializer. For example, we could define a second `list2` constructor that initializes its base class by copying the value of an existing
`list` object.

```
extern list &exlist;

list2::list2( list2 *bl ) : list( exlist ) {
     link = bl;
}
```

The arguments supplied to the base class constructor in the member initialization list of the original `list2` constructor are of type `ETYPE` and
`list2 *`, whereas the types expected by the `list` constructor are `ETYPE`
and `list *`. Why isn't it an error to initialize a `list *` with a
`list2 *`? The reason is that an object of class `list2` is also an object
of class `list`. This is what we specify when we derive one class from
another. Additionally, if a class `Base` is a *public* base class of another
class `Derived`, then there is a predefined conversion from a `Derived` to
a `Base`, from a pointer to a `Derived` to a pointer to a `Base`, and from a
reference to a `Derived` to a reference to a `Base`. We say that a
`Derived` *is a* `Base` in many contexts. These conversions do not exist if
`Base` is a private base class of `Derived`.

This "is a" concept is a powerful abstraction mechanism, in that it allows derived classes to be treated as base classes in many contexts. For example, because `list` is a public base class of `list2`, we can call the
`print_list` function of the previous chapter with either a list composed
of `list`s or a list composed of `list2`s.

```
typedef int ETYPE;
void
print_list( list *lst ) {
    extern void print( int );
    for( list *p = lst; p; p = p->next() )
        print( p->value() );
}

main() {
    list *lp = new list( 1, 0 );
    lp = new list( 2, lp );
    lp = new list( 3, lp );
    print_list( lp );

    list2 *l2p = new list2( 1, 0, 0 );
    l2p = new list2( 2, l2p, 0 );
    l2p = new list2( 3, l2p, 0 );
    print_list( l2p );
}
```

In some cases a derived class may just add or modify behavior of its base class. For instance, in the previous chapter we used the String data type to create a pathname for a file and open it. We can encapsulate this behavior in a class derived from String.

The abstract operations we want to perform on pathnames are creation, concatenation, and comparison of the character strings that represent the pathname, as well as an open operation on the files to which they refer. Many of these operations are provided in the String type, and a pathname can be viewed as either an augmentation or a special case of String. When we say, "A pathname is a String with the following additional properties . . . ," we are thinking of an augmented String. When we say, "A pathname is a kind of String that . . ." we are thinking of a special case of a String. Whichever of these conceptualizations we use, we express it with class derivation.

```
class Pathname : public String {
  public:
    friend
    Pathname &operator +( Pathname &, Pathname & );
    FILE *open();
};
```

In this case, we are not adding any data members to what Pathname inherits from String, we are just adding behavior. In this sense a Pathname is simply a String viewed from a different perspective.

We inherit the abstract operations of creation, destruction, comparison, and so forth, unchanged from `String`. For concatenation, however, it is necessary to separate two sequences of directory names with a slash.

```
Pathname &
operator +( Pathname &p1, Pathname &p2 ) {
    return (String &)p1 + "/" + (String &)p2;
}
```

`Pathname::open` attempts to open the file referred to by the `String` representation of the pathname.

```
FILE *
Pathname::open() {
    return fopen( *this, "r+" );
}
```

The `Pathname` actual argument to `fopen` is converted to a `char *` by the `operator char *` inherited from class `String`.

```
extern char *home_dir, *path, *file;
Pathname home = home_dir;
Pathname file = home + path + file;
FILE *fp = file->open();
```

This example exemplifies one of the central ideas in using derived classes: inherit most of a class's behavior from base classes, and add to base class behavior only when necessary. Inheritance used in this way is an effective technique for sharing and reusing code.

5.2 Class Hierarchies

Many problems are not easily modeled as distinct types but are more naturally represented as collections of related types. For example, a node for a compiler abstract syntax tree may have to represent a variety of programming language constructs. Each of these types of node shares a common core of properties with the others (those properties that make them nodes), but each kind of node has additional properties that distinguish it from the others. Using only data abstraction to represent all node types gives us the choice of creating either a single type that incorporates the complexities of all the others, or a set of distinct types that does not reflect their commonality. A better approach is to use class derivation to create a set of node types related by inheritance.

We approach this problem by creating a hierarchy of node types. The base class types in the hierarchy provide the common structure and functionality, and, conversely, the derived class types provide specialized versions of their base classes.

Suppose we are designing an abstract syntax tree for a calculator program. Each internal node of the tree represents an operation to be performed, and each leaf represents a value. For example, the expression $-5+12*4$ would be represented as

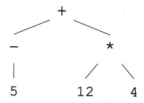

if the operators +, *, and unary − have the same precedences in our calculator language as they do in C++.

We start by defining a general node type that serves as a base class for all other node types.

```
class Node {
   public:
      enum {
          PLUS,
          TIMES,
          UMINUS,
          INT
      };
      const int code;
      Node( int c ) : code(c) {}
      int eval();
};
```

Node contains a code that identifies the actual type of node: +, *, unary − or integer, a constructor, and a member function to evaluate an abstract syntax tree.

We use class derivation to create distinct node types from Node for the operators +, *, and unary −, and for the integer values at the leaves of the tree. The derived class constructors explicitly invoke the base class constructor and supply the appropriate node code.

```
class Plus : public Node {
  public:
    Node *left, *right;
    Plus( Node *l, Node *r ) : Node(PLUS)
        { left = l; right = r; }
};

class Times : public Node {
  public:
    Node *left, *right;
    Times( Node *l, Node *r ) : Node(TIMES)
        { left = l; right = r; }
};

class Uminus : public Node {
  public:
    Node *operand;
    Uminus( Node *o ) : Node(UMINUS)
        { operand = o; }
};


class Int : public Node {
  public:
    int value;
    Int( int v ) : Node(INT)
        { value = v; }
};
```

This arrangement is not too bad, although there is a lot of duplication
between the two binary operators. As more binary operators are added to
our calculator language this duplication becomes unwieldy and a potential
source of errors. It is better to introduce another level of derivation that reflects their commonality.

```
class Binop : public Node {
  public:
    Node *left, *right;
    Binop( int c, Node *l, Node *r ) : Node(c)
        { left = l; right = r; }
};

class Plus : public Binop {
  public:
    Plus( Node *l, Node *r ) : Binop(PLUS, l, r) {}
};
```

```
class Times : public Binop {
  public:
    Times( Node *l, Node *r ) : Binop(TIMES, l, r) {}
};
```

The resulting hierarchy of class types shows how node types are related by inheritance.

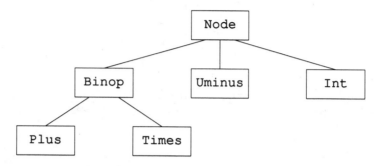

Thus a Plus is both a Binop and a Node, but not a Uminus. An Int is a Node but not a Binop, and so forth. If we have been careful in the design of our class hierarchy, these inheritance relationships between types should match our intuition about the concepts they represent in the problem domain. Inheritance is a conceptual aid as well as a method for code factoring and sharing.

```
int
Node::eval() {
    switch( code ) {
    case INT:
        return ((Int *)this)->value;
    case UMINUS:
        return -((Uminus *)this)->operand->eval();
    case PLUS:
        return ((Binop *)this)->left->eval()
               + ((Binop *)this)->right->eval();
    case TIMES:
        return ((Binop *)this)->left->eval()
               * ((Binop *)this)->right->eval();
    default:
        error();
        return 0;
    }
}
```

Here we have implemented Node::eval by switching on Node::code and recursively evaluating subtrees. In order to call the correct eval member function, we have to cast the `this` pointer to the appropriate derived type object as indicated by the value of the node code. Because each class object of a type derived from `Node` is also a `Node`, a pointer to a `Node` is also a pointer to an object of the derived class indicated by `Node::code`. Casting the `this` pointer to the corresponding pointer to derived class type allows us to access the derived class members and perform the evaluation.

This is not too bad in this limited case, but one could hardly describe it as a natural solution to the problem. It is easy to see how this approach could get out of hand in more complex situations, when one is forced to identify explicitly the correct `eval` routine before invocation.

Although our design works—we can build and evaluate abstract syntax trees—there is a major flaw in our implementation. We have implemented a hierarchy of node types, but in using an explicit node code, class `Node` essentially defines what node types can be derived from it.

The problem is obvious when we add a new type of node to the hierarchy. For example, if we want to add a divide operator, it is not sufficient simply to declare a class type derived from `Binop`. We must also change the implementation of `Node::eval` (and presumably add a new element to the enumeration of class `Node`). If the existing node hierarchy were part of a library, our users would be forced to copy and edit it to produce their own private version. In so doing they would be putting themselves in the position of either tracking changes to the library in their private version or diverging from the standard library. In either case, our goal in providing a library will not have been met.

A better approach is to encapsulate node-specific information entirely within the appropriate node, without recording any node-specific information in node types higher up in the hierarchy. To do this effectively, we have to be able to distinguish between node types at runtime more effectively than we do in the current implementation of `Node::eval`, where we use a node code and explicit casts. We accomplish this with virtual functions.

5.3 Virtual Functions

Let us leave our abstract syntax tree example for awhile and look at a simple example.

Suppose we are dealing with a collection of fruit types related by inheritance.

```
class fruit {
  public:
    char *identify() { return "fruit"; }
};

class apple : public fruit {
  public:
    char *identify() { return "apple"; }
};

class orange : public fruit {
  public:
    char *identify() { return "orange"; }
};
```

Our application is to create a heterogeneous list of fruit objects and have each list element identify itself. We use the singly linked list node type described earlier in this chapter.

```
typedef fruit *ETYPE;
#include "list.h"

void
print_list( list *lst ) {
    extern void print( char * );
    while( lst ) {
        print( lst->value()->identify() );
        lst = lst->next();
    }
}


main() {
    list *lst = new list( new fruit, 0 );
    lst = new list( new apple, lst );
    lst = new list( new orange, lst );
    print_list( lst );
}
```

This program prints the word "fruit" three times even though the list contains an orange, an apple, and a fruit. This behavior is correct because the expression lst->value() is of type fruit *, and fruit::identify returns a pointer to the character string "fruit". Ordinarily the member function called depends on the type of the pointer or reference used to access it, not the actual type of the object to which the pointer or reference refers.

```
fruit *fp = new apple;
fp->identify(); // returns "fruit"
((apple *)fp)->identify();  // returns "apple"
apple *ap = (apple *)fp;
ap->identify(); // returns "apple"
```

Compare this to the implementation of `Node::eval` earlier in this chapter.

For our fruit identification program, however, we would like the proper identify function to be determined by the actual object type, not by the type of the pointer or reference used to access the object. For this we use virtual functions.

```
class fruit {
  public:
    virtual char *identify() { return "fruit"; }
};
```

Virtual functions allow derived classes to provide alternative versions for a base class function. In declaring `fruit::identify` to be virtual, we are saying that classes derived from `fruit` are expected to have their own versions of `identify`, and that these functions should be invoked based on the actual object types. Thus an `apple` or an `orange` will have its own version of the virtual function invoked for it, even when it is being treated as a `fruit`.

Having added the keyword `virtual` to the declaration of `fruit::identify`, our program now runs as we want it to, printing "orange", "apple", "fruit".

Notice that `apple::identify` and `orange::identify` are virtual without our having explicitly declared them to be so (although we could have). The rules for determining when a function is virtual are simple: a function is virtual if it is declared virtual, or if there is a base class function with the same signature that is virtual. A function's signature is composed of its name and its formal argument types. For example, if the declaration of `apple::identify` were

```
char *identify( int = 0 );
```

then it would not be virtual, because it would then have a different signature than `fruit::identify`. The output of our program in this case would be "orange", "fruit", "fruit". If the signature of a derived class member function matches that of a base class virtual member, then the return type must also match that of the base class function. This ensures that the dynamic (runtime) binding provided by virtual functions is type safe.

The combination of the "is a" relationship from a derived class to its public base and dynamic binding of virtual functions is a very useful abstraction method. For example, our `print_list` function deals only with lists of `fruit` pointers. We can construct a hierarchy of types of arbitrary complexity and depth based on class `fruit` without having to alter the implementation of `print_list`. For example, we could widen the hierarchy by adding a `banana` type derived from `fruit`, or extend the hierarchy downward by deriving `macintosh` and `delicious` from `apple`. Inheritance used in this way allows us to abstract commonality from a group of related types and write general routines based on our abstraction. Type-specific details of derived types are encapsulated within the types.

Using these concepts, we can now redesign our abstract syntax tree implementation to take advantage of virtual functions.

```
class Node {
  public:
    Node() {}
    virtual ~Node() {}
    virtual int eval() { error(); return 0; }
};

class Binop : public Node {
  public:
    Node *left, *right;
    ~Binop() { delete left; delete right; }
    Binop( Node *l, Node *r ) { left = l; right = r; }
};

class Plus : public Binop {
  public:
    Plus( Node *l, Node *r ) : Binop(l,r) {}
    int eval() { return left->eval() + right->eval(); }
};

class Times : public Binop {
  public:
    Times( Node *l, Node *r ) : Binop(l,r) {}
    int eval() { return left->eval() * right->eval(); }
};
```

```
class Uminus : public Node {
    Node *operand;
  public:
    Uminus( Node *o ) { operand = o; }
    ~Uminus() { delete operand; }
    int eval() { return -operand->eval(); }
};

class Int : public Node {
    int value;
  public:
    Int( int v ) { value = v; }
    int eval() { return value; }
};
```

eval is declared to be virtual in Node, so the evals in Plus, Times, Uminus, and Int are also virtual. Binop does not declare an eval function, so a Binop object invokes Node::eval, inherited from its Node base class. Now we can create and evaluate abstract syntax trees.

```
int
limited_use() {
    // evaluate -5+12*4
    Node *np =
        new Plus(
            new Uminus(
                new Int( 5 ),
            ),
            new Times(
                new Int( 12 ),
                new Int( 4 )
            )
        );
    int result = np->eval();
    delete np;
    return result;
}
```

The virtual call of eval invokes Plus::eval, because a Plus node is at the root of the abstract syntax tree pointed to by np. Plus::eval invokes the virtual eval functions for its left and right subtrees, which in this case results in calls to Uminus::eval and Times::eval, respectively, and so on. At each step, the actual function invoked is determined by the type of the node at the root of the subtree being evaluated.

Class Node also declares a virtual destructor. Although a destructor cannot be called explicitly, in the way that a member function can, it can be invoked in a virtual manner. The line

```
    delete np;
```

invokes the virtual destructor for the root of the abstract syntax tree pointed to by np. This is a Plus node, which defines no destructor, so the inherited destructor Binop::~Binop is invoked instead. Binop::~Binop invokes the virtual destructors for its left and right subtrees, and so on. The result is that the single delete expression frees the entire abstract syntax tree.

As an aside, note that constructors cannot be virtual. A constructor creates an object, whereas a virtual function requires an already existing object to determine what function to call.

The use of virtual functions allows us to encapsulate node-specific operations within the declaration of a specific node type. We can now add new node types to the hierarchy without affecting existing code.

```
    class Div : public Binop {
      public:
        Div( Node *l, Node *r ) : Binop(l,r) {}
        int eval() { return left->eval()
                            / right->eval(); }
    };
```

Having declared class Div, we can create and evaluate Div objects as nodes in an abstract syntax tree without changing the implementations of the other node types.

5.4 Protected Members

Node::eval serves a dual role. It is both the "root" virtual function that causes all the other eval members with the same signature to be virtual and a kind of stopgap. If we had forgotten to declare a Div::eval, any attempt to invoke eval for a Div node would result in a call to Node::eval and an error. No Binop or Node objects should be created or evaluated, only objects of classes derived from them. A stopgap function at the root of the hierarchy is an effective way of catching errors of this kind, but unfortunately the error is not evident until runtime, and only then if such a node is actually evaluated.

It is preferable (and safer) to prevent users of the node hierarchy from creating objects of these types at all. One way to do this is to make the constructors for Node and Binop private. Unfortunately, this will also prevent classes derived from them from using the constructors.

```
class Node {
    Node() {}
  public:
    // ...
};

class Int : public Node {
    int value;
  public:
    Int( int v ) {
        // error!  Implicit invocation of
        // private Node::Node
// ...
```

A similar problem arises with the members `left` and `right` of class
`Binop`. We would prefer that they were private to protect them from abuse
by casual users of the node hierarchy, but they must be public in order that
classes derived from `Binop` (`Plus`, `Times`, and `Div`) can use them.

We solve this problem with protected class members. A sequence of
protected members is introduced in a class definition by the syntax
`protected:`, just as public members can be introduced by `public:`,
and private members by `private:`. A protected member is like a private
member, except that it can be accessed by members and friends of classes
derived from the class in which it is declared. Similar to public members, a
base class's protected members are protected in the derived class if the base
is public, and private otherwise.

```
class Node {
  protected:
    Node() {}
  public:
    virtual ~Node() {}
    virtual int eval();
};

class Binop : public Node {
  protected:
    Node *left, *right;
    Binop( Node *l, Node *r )
        { left = l; right = r; }
    ~Binop() { delete left; delete right; }
};
```

Now only members and friends of `Node`, `Binop`, and classes derived from
them can invoke their constructors, so other code cannot allocate nodes of
those types. Additionally, `Binop::left` and `Binop::right` can be

accessed only by members and friends of binary operators derived from it.

5.5   Inheritance as a Design Tool

Inheritance is a design method in that it allows one to abstract a problem to its most general form in a base class at the root of a hierarchy, and model and write code dealing only with the abstraction. Specialized cases (which may themselves be abstractions of even more specialized cases) can then be handled with classes derived from the base class.

For example, in the abstract syntax tree example we started with a general concept of node, and successively expanded the node type hierarchy by specialization. The original abstraction remains, however. In code like

```
void
print_value( Node *np ) {
    extern void print( int );
    print( np->eval() );
}
```

we are dealing only with Nodes, and the complexities of the specialized types derived from Node remain hidden from general-purpose routines.

As a design tool, the use of inheritance is similar to that of stepwise refinement of the function decomposition paradigm described in Chapter 2. Stepwise refinement divides the procedural aspects of a problem into a hierarchy of procedures, whereas inheritance divides the type aspects of a problem into a hierarchy of types.

Although the result of developing a program by stepwise refinement is a strict hierarchy of procedures, one does not necessarily arrive at that result in a strictly top-down fashion. Sometimes low-level procedures are coded first to see how their implementation affects the structure of procedures higher in the hierarchy.

In a similar way, in a complex program that deals with many different types it may not be obvious how the types are related to each other, if at all. Sometimes it is only after having coded the implementations of several seemingly disparate types that their commonality is evident. Inheritance can then be used to share the common parts of their interface and implementation. Frequently this commonality is evidence of a deeper abstraction, and the "discovered" inheritance hierarchy becomes a working design abstraction.

Consider as a meta-example the implementation of a symbol table for a

C++ compiler. In the interest of brevity we will simplify a bit, but the general framework of the solution could be (and has been) used to develop a symbol table for a C++ compiler.

Let us review the basics of scope in C++. Scope in C++ is essentially block-structured. That is, a name is defined from its point of first appearance to the end of the block in which it is defined. The appearance of a name in an inner block hides all names with the same identifier defined in outer blocks. For the purpose of symbol management, the file itself can be considered to be a block.

Member functions and inheritance increase the complexity of this simple block structure, however. The enclosing scope of a member function is the scope of the class of which it is a member.

```
int i;
class C {
    int i;
    f() { i = 1; }
};
```

The member function f assigns to the class member i, not the global i. The following fragment is equivalent to the previous one:

```
int i;
class C {
    int i;
    inline f();
};
C::f() { i = 1; }
```

The enclosing scope of a member function is its class whether or not it is textually enclosed within the class.

The enclosing scope of a derived class is its base class. For example:

```
class B { public: int i; };
int i;
void g() {
    int i;
    class D1 : public B {
        f() { i = 1; }
    };
}
class D2 : public B {};
```

Classes B, D1, and D2, form a class hierarchy in which B is the enclosing scope for both D1 and D2. In particular, note that the enclosing scope for D1 is not the scope of the function g. Thus the member function f of D1 assigns to the base class member i, not the local or file scope i.

As a first approach to the design of the symbol table, we decide to represent the various flavors of scope (global, class, function) as separate tables rather than maintain a single monolithic structure. We represent each kind of table as a separate class with member functions for lookup and insertion of names. In addition, because the scope of a derived class is nested within that of its base class, the class table type has a member function that returns a pointer to its base class's table.

```
class Gtab {
  public:
    name *insert( char * );
    name *lookup( char * );
};

class Ctab {
  public:
    name *insert( char * );
    name *lookup( char * );
    Ctab *base_class();
};

class Ftab {
  public:
    name *insert( char * );
    name *lookup( char * );
};
```

In each case the argument to the insertion or lookup function is a pointer to an identifier, and the return value is a symbol table name. For purposes of this illustration, we consider a name to be a structure with a pointer to its identifier and possibly other information.

Having partitioned our problem into three separate cases, we are free to implement each table's semantics in whatever way is most appropriate to each case. For instance, we may have developed a heuristic that indicates a class table is best organized as a list, the global table as a simple hash table, and a function table as a more complex hash table that keeps track of block scope within the function. The single global table might be structured as follows:

```
class Gtab {
    static name *t[ 256 ];
    int hash( char * );
  public:
    name *insert( char * );
    name *lookup( char * );
} gtable;
```

At this point we have a complete representation for a given scope. We use the rules we outlined at the start of this example to find the enclosing scope. We start by declaring three "current scope" pointers, one for each kind of symbol table.

```
Gtab *gptr; // points to global table
Ctab *cptr; // points to current class table
Ftab *fptr; // points to current function table
```

However, although this approach will work, it makes the code to do simple insertions and lookups rather complex.

```
name *
lookup( char *id ) {
    name *n;
    if( fptr )
        if( n = fptr->lookup( id ) )
            return n;
    for( Ctab *cp = cptr; cp; cp = cp->base_class() )
        if( n = cp->lookup( id ) )
            return n;
    return gptr->lookup( id );
}

name *
insert( char *id ) {
    if( fptr )
        return fptr->insert( id );
    if( cptr )
        return cptr->insert( id );
    return gptr->insert( id );
}
```

Under this scheme, we must always distinguish between specific types of scope even in situations when we are performing generic operations.

An alternate approach is to recognize the commonality of these three symbol table types and use inheritance to make the commonality explicit.

```
class Tab {
  protected:
    Tab *parent;
  public:
    virtual name *insert( char * );
    virtual name *look( char * );
};

class Gtab : public Tab { /* ... */ };
class Ctab : public Tab { /* ... */ };
class Ftab : public Tab { /* ... */ };
```

Here we represent the enclosing scope explicitly as a pointer to the Tab type at the root of the symbol table hierarchy. Because Tab is a public base class of Gtab, Ctab, and Ftab, Tab::parent can refer to any symbol table object. To keep track of the current scope, we use a global variable of type Tab *, curr_tab, to point to the current table.

At this point we have a workable framework for our C++ symbol table. At any given time the state of scope consists of the ensemble of the individual function and class tables, and the global table. The relationships among these tables are represented by their parent pointers.

When a new scope comes into existence, say at the beginning of a class body, we create a new class table and initialize it to refer to the proper enclosing scope. For instance, if the class is a derived class, it occurs in the scope of its base class, so parent refers to the base class table. If the class is not derived, then its parent is the global table (regardless of whether it is lexically nested in a function or another class). Rewritten to take advantage of the table hierarchy and virtual functions it makes possible, the general lookup routine becomes noticeably simpler.

```
name *
lookup( char * id ) {
    name *n;
    for( Tab *t = curr_tab; t; t = t->parent )
        if( n = t->look( id ) )
            return n;
    return 0;
}
```

In a similar way insertions are simplified, and

```
curr_tab->insert( id );
```

inserts a name with identifier id in the current table, whether it's global, class, or function.

Having expressed the relationship of our three original symbol table

types as special cases of a general table type, we have not only simplified
use of the types, but in developing an abstraction of a symbol table, we
have simplified the way we *think* about the types.

5.6   Inheritance for Interface Sharing

In some of the examples in this chapter, derived classes are augmenta-
tions or specializations of base classes that are fully usable types in their
own right. Note that list2 is derived from list, and Pathname from
String, but both list and String are perfectly functional types. On
the other hand, the base Tab type of our symbol table hierarchy and Node
of our abstract syntax tree node hierarchy are not fully functional, and require that their definition be completed by class derivation. Therefore Tab
and Node form a kind of partial type, half implementation and half template, that is completed in classes derived from them.

We can extend this concept, and define a base class that serves strictly as
a template for classes derived from it, in order to guarantee that a derived
type satisfies a certain interface. Here we would regard a derived class not
as an augmentation or specialization of its base class but rather as a realiza-
tion of the interface specified by its base class.

Consider the task of specifying the interface between the kernel and a
device driver in the UNIX operating system. To issue a system call to
open, close, read, write, and so on, a given device, the kernel indexes a
two-dimensional device switch table with a major device number and a code
corresponding to the type of system call (such as open or close). The major
device number specifies a kind of device (such as disk or terminal) and a
minor device number is used to distinguish actual devices of the same type
(such as multiple disks or multiple terminals). The table contains function
addresses corresponding to the device, operation pair used to index the
table. The kernel completes the system call by calling the appropriate routine indirectly through the device switch table.

This switch table defines the interface between the UNIX kernel and the
device driver routines. There are drawbacks to the scheme, however. First,
the dimensions and content of the table are fixed when the kernel is built
(compiled) and adding a new type of device requires that the kernel be re-
built. Second, there is no guarantee that the functions whose addresses are
in the switch table have the correct types. Third, information relating to a
specific kind of device is dispersed in several different places and doesn't
help us to reason about the device as an entity in itself.

An alternative way to implement the interface is to define a device driver type that encapsulates the behavior of a generic device driver.

```
class Device {
  public:
    virtual int open(char *, int, int);
    virtual int close(int);
    virtual int read(int, char *, unsigned);
    virtual int write(int, char *, unsigned);
    virtual int ioctl(int, int ...);
    Device();
    ~Device();
};
```

These generic device driver member functions implement default behavior.

```
int
Device::open( char *path, int oflag, int mode ) {
    return nulldev();
}
```

Now the kernel can deal with all devices through this generic device type, just as we earlier evaluated all abstract syntax tree node types through a generic Node type, and accessed all symbol tables through a generic Tab type.

We create a type for a specific kind of device driver by derivation from this template.

```
class Terminal : public Device {
  public:
    int open(char *, int, int);
    int close(int);
    int read(int, char *, unsigned);
    int write(int, char *, unsigned);
    int ioctl(int, int ...);
    Terminal();
    ~Terminal();
};
```

Any part of the interface not explicitly redefined in the derived device type defaults to the routine in the base type.

```
class Mem_mapped_io : public Device {
  public:
    int read(int, char *, unsigned);
    int write(int, char *, unsigned);
    int ioctl(int, int ...);
};
```

The device driver hierarchy replaces the device switch table. We can think of the individual derived device types as replacing the major device numbers and the dynamic binding provided by virtual functions as replacing the switch table. To replace the minor device numbers, we create a device object for each physical device of a given type. For instance, if there are five disk drives attached to the backplane, there are a corresponding five disk objects being managed by the kernel; every time a user logs on to the system, a corresponding terminal object is created and destroyed when that user logs off.

5.7   Multiple Inheritance

A derived class can have any number of base classes. The use of two or more base classes is called multiple inheritance. Although the uses of multiple inheritance are less common than those of single inheritance, multiple inheritance is useful for creating class types that combine the behavior of two or more other class types.

For example, we may want to create a type that monitors a given condition and displays its status on the screen. Suppose we have a bit-map graphics library available with a dial abstract data type that displays a changing value.

```
class Dial {
    // irrelevant implementation details...
  protected:
    double value;
    Dial( char *, double, double );
    ~Dial();
};
```

The `Dial` constructor displays a dial with the argument label, and with measurement range between the values of the second and third arguments. After creation, a `Dial` object continuously displays the current value of `Dial::value`.

We also have available a sampler type.

```
class Sampler {
    // implementation details...
  protected:
    double freq;
    virtual void sample();
    Sampler( double );
    ~Sampler();
};
```

A `Sampler` object simply invokes its virtual `sample` function every `Sampler::freq` seconds.

Our monitor type is both a `Dial` and a `Sampler`. We express this by using multiple inheritance to inherit from both classes.

```
class Monitor : public Sampler, public Dial {
    void sample() { value = get_value(); }
  protected:
    virtual double get_value();
    Monitor( char *lab, double l, double h, double f )
        : Dial( lab, l, h ), Sampler( f ) {}
};
```

The syntax

```
class Monitor : public Sampler, public Dial
```

declares `Monitor` to be a new class type derived from both `Dial` and `Sampler`. The use of multiple base classes is a natural extension of the single inheritance case of a single base class. Any number of class names can be present on the comma-separated base class list, but no name can appear twice on the same list.

The `Monitor` constructor uses a member initialization list to invoke the base class constructors explicitly. The order of initialization is as specified by the member initialization list, with any implicit base class initializations being invoked in the order the base classes appear on the base class list in the class definition. Recall that base classes are always initialized before members, even if a member name occurs before a base class name on a member initialization list.

The scope of class `Monitor` "nests" within the scopes of *both* its base classes. Therefore `Monitor::sample` is a virtual function that redefines `Sampler::sample`. The reference to `value` in `Monitor::sample` refers to `Dial::value`.

This "multiple nesting" can be a source of ambiguities that do not occur under single inheritance. To illustrate some of these problems, let us return to our hierarchy of fruit types and also include a hierarchy of tree types.

```
class fruit {
  public:
    virtual char *identify() { return "fruit"; }
};

class tree {
  public:
    virtual char *identify() { return "tree"; }
};
```

Some types are both `fruit` and `tree`.

```
class apple : public fruit, public tree {};

apple *ap = new apple;
ap->identify(); // error!
```

The code does not compile because the function call is ambiguous. Because the scope of `apple` nests in the scopes of both `fruit` and `tree`, the call could refer to either `fruit::identify` or `tree::identify`. We can make the call unambiguous by being explicit about the base class to which we refer, either by using the scope operator

```
ap->fruit::identify();
```

or a cast:

```
((fruit *)ap)->identify();
```

A better solution is to define an `identify` function for class `apple` with the desired behavior.

```
class apple : public fruit, public tree {
  public:
    char *identify() { return "apple"; }
};
// ...
ap->identify(); // unambiguous
```

All the usual relationships hold between a derived class and each of its base classes under multiple inheritance as they would with a single base class. For instance, `apple::identify` is a virtual function that redefines both `tree::identify` and `fruit::identify`. Additionally, because both `fruit` and `tree` are public base classes of `apple`, there are predefined conversions from `apple` to both `fruit` and `tree`.

```
apple a;
tree &t = a;     // OK, an apple is a tree
fruit *f = &a;   // OK, an apple is a fruit
*f = t;          // error! a tree is not a fruit
a = t;           // error! a fruit is not an apple
```

Compare the above to the conversions described earlier for the abstract syntax tree node hierarchy.

Let us return to our `Monitor` class. Using multiple inheritance we have combined two separate concepts, a `Dial` and a `Sampler`, to produce a new type. This use of multiple inheritance for combining types is a very important one.

Now we can derive specialized monitor types from class `Monitor`. A type derived from `Monitor` has to provide initializing values to be passed through the `Monitor` constructor to the `Dial` and `Sampler` classes, as well as define a function that provides the value to be monitored.

```
class Mem_usage : public Monitor {
    char *start;
    char *max;
  public:
    double get_value() {
        return (current_top()-start)/(max-start);
    }
    Mem_usage() : Monitor("Memory Usage",0,100,0.1),
            start( current_top() ),
            max( get_limit() ) {}
};
```

A `Mem_usage` object monitors the percent of available memory in use by the process in which it occurs. The virtual `get_value` function returns the fraction of available memory used from the time the `Mem_usage` object was created. A system function, here called `current_top`, provides the top memory address of the process for the calculation in `get_value`. The constructor labels the monitor dial "Memory Usage", sets the displayed range of values between `0.0` and `100.0`, and sets the sampling rate to ten times per second. Note that `current_top` is used again to record the starting top memory address of the process. Another system function, called `get_limit`, provides the maximum address to which the process memory is allowed to grow.

As another (rather less serious) example, suppose we want to monitor the velocity of a mouse attached to our terminal. We assume we have available the usual bit-map graphic types (perhaps from the same library in which the

Dial type is defined) and objects like Point (a screen position in Cartesian coordinates) and Mouse (an object representing the mouse).

```
class Mouse_velocity : public Monitor {
    Point prev;
  public:
    double get_value() {
        extern const int PIXELS_PER_INCH;
        double value = dist( Mouse.abs_pos, prev )
                    / (freq * PIXELS_PER_INCH);
        prev = Mouse.abs_pos;
        return value;
    }
    Mouse_velocity() :
        Monitor( "Velocity", 0, 120, .01 ) {
        prev = Mouse.abs_pos;
    }
};
```

A Mouse_velocity object displays the current velocity of the mouse in inches per second. Notice that the virtual get_value function refers to freq, a member of Sampler, which is two levels of inheritance away.

5.8   Virtual Base Classes

The Monitor type uses multiple inheritance to combine two entirely distinct classes. Multiple inheritance can also be used to combine more closely related classes, however. For example, we might want to create a new device type that has properties from two existing device types.

```
class Monitored_device :
    public Device, public Monitor {
    // ...
};

class Network_device :
    public Device, public Protocol {
    // ...
};
```

A Monitored_device monitors the transmission rate of data through a device, and a Network_device is an interface to a network driver board that obeys a given network protocol. We would like to create a new device type that monitors a network transmission rate. We could construct a new device type ''from scratch'',

```
class Monitored_network_device :
    public Device, public Monitor, public Protocol {
    // ...
};
```

but we wouldn't be able to use our new type as a Network_device or a Monitored_device, because there would then be no inheritance relation between the types.

The alternative of deriving from the two existing devices would cause two Device base classes to appear in the hierarchy.

```
class Monitored_network_device :
    public Monitored_device, public Network_device {
    // ...
};
```

In some cases this is just what is required, but it is not what we need for our new device type. First, any simple attempt to use the new type as a device would result in ambiguity errors, and we would always have to specify the instance of Device to which we were referring.

```
Monitored_network_device iso;
iso.open( "/dev/iso", O_RDWR, 0 );
            // error! ambiguous
iso.Device::open( "/dev/iso", O_RDWR, 0 );
            // error! still ambiguous
iso.Network_device::open( "/dev/iso", O_RDWR, 0 );
            // OK, Network_device's Device
iso.Monitored_device::open( "/dev/iso", O_RDWR, 0 );
            // OK, Monitored_device's Device
```

A more basic problem is that, although we are dealing with a single physical device, our type contains two separate representations of it. This is bound to cause difficulties. For instance, because the Device constructor would be activated twice for each Monitored_network_device object, the operating system kernel, which deals with devices entirely through the interface provided by the Device type, would probably conclude that there are two devices where there is only one.

What we would like to do is create a class that is derived from both Monitored_device and Network_device, but that has only a single instance of Device. We accomplish this with virtual base classes.

```
class Monitored_device :
    public virtual Device, public Monitor {
    // ...
};

class Network_device :
    public virtual Device, public Protocol {
    // ...
};

class Monitored_network_device :
    public Monitored_device, public Network_device {
    // ...
};
```

In declaring a base class virtual we are saying that we want its representation to be shared with every other virtual occurrence of that base class in an object. There is only a single occurrence of `Device` in the class `Monitored_network_device` because both occurrences of `Device` are declared to be virtual. Because there is only a single `Device`, unqualified references to its members are no longer ambiguous.

```
iso.open( "/dev/iso", O_RDWR, 0 );   // unambiguous
```

Likewise, the `Device` constructor is invoked only once for a `Monitored_network_device` object, because there is only one `Device` to initialize.

There are some restrictions associated with the use of virtual base classes. First, a base class that is virtual cannot be explicitly initialized by appearing on a constructor's member initialization list. Because a class that has a constructor must be initialized, this implies that a class that is used as a virtual base class must either have no constructor or must have a constructor that can be invoked with no arguments. Any (implicit) initialization of virtual base classes is done before any other base class, including those that are explicitly initialized on the member initialization list. A second restriction involves casting: it is illegal to cast a pointer to a virtual base class to a pointer to a class (directly or indirectly) derived from it.

5.9 Exercises

Exercise 5-1. Consider the coordinate pair and polar implementations of class `complex` of the previous chapter. Could they be implemented as distinct types related by inheritance and used together? Is this an appropriate use of inheritance? ☐

Exercise 5-2. Consider the graph and finite state automaton abstract data types from the exercises of the previous chapter. Can one be derived from the other? Can they share a common base class? How would you characterize each of these uses of inheritance, as code sharing only, or is there a conceptual commonality between graphs and finite state automata? ☐

Exercise 5-3. †Add identifier and assignment node types to the calculator abstract syntax tree node hierarchy. Do you have to change the implementation of the other node types to do this? Use the resulting node hierarchy to write a complete, interactive calculator program. ☐

Exercise 5-4. In the implementation of `operator +` (concatenation) for the `Pathname` type, what would happen if we didn't cast the two `Pathname&` arguments to `String&`? (Hint: Which version of `operator +` is called with the casts in place, and which would be called without the casts?) ☐

Exercise 5-5. Suppose there was an existing hardware interface library for terminal devices with the following inheritance hierarchy:

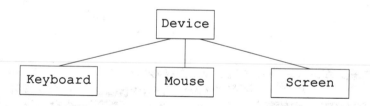

Suppose you could not modify the library and had to add tablet and light pen types into the hierarchy. Where and how would you add them? Suppose you could modify the library. How would you add the types now? How would you restructure the hierarchy to ease the introduction of new types in the future? ☐

Exercise 5-6. Show how inheritance can be used to package and supply a set of constants to other class types. ☐

Exercise 5-7. Use the `Monitor` type to create class types that monitor a) typing speed, b) system load, c) the number of users logged on to the system, †d) number of abstract syntax tree nodes allocated, and e) relative percentage of binary operator nodes to unary operator nodes. ☐

Exercise 5-8. Show how inheritance can be used to provide different "views" of a given base class. Design a database record for an employee database and supply derived class views appropriate for a) general use, b) payroll, c) supervision, and d) the FBI. □

CHAPTER 6: **Object-Oriented Programming**

Procedural programming techniques focus on the algorithms used to solve a problem, leaving the data structures that are acted on by functions as separate parts of the program organization. In contrast, object-oriented programming focuses on the domain of the problem for which the program is written: the elements of the program design correspond to objects in the problem description. The general approach of object-oriented programming is to define a collection of object types. Object types are modules that integrate the data structures that represent the elements of the problem with the operations needed to produce a solution. Once these object types are defined, instances of objects for the specific problem are created, and operations are invoked to do the processing.

In C++, classes serve as object types, and member functions provide the means for building operations into the type.

6.1 Designing in Objects

Object-oriented program design is an extension of the use of data abstraction. The abstract data types, or object types, not only hide the structure of data but encapsulate all the processing as operations on objects. The essence of object-oriented design is finding the most suitable object types.

Before discussing some guidelines for designing object types, let's look at two object-oriented programs that sort a list of integers. To focus on the design, we won't show the details of the implementations. The first program uses an `Intlist` abstract data type that contains operators to sort and output the list. Integers are read into the list when an `Intlist` object is created.

```
class Intlist {
    // etc.
public:
    Intlist();
    sort();
    write();
};

main() {
    Intlist *ilist = new Intlist();
    ilist->sort();
    ilist->write();
}
```

The other program uses a Sortedintlist abstract data type, which reads in integers in the process of creating a sorted list. Sortedintlist contains an operator for output.

```
class Sortedintlist {
    // etc.
public:
    Sortedintlist();
    write();
};

main() {
    Sortedintlist *slist = new Sortedintlist();
    slist->write();
}
```

Which of these has the better design, or are they equally good?

A good guideline for designing object types is to look for nouns and verbs in the description of the problem to be solved. The nouns become objects in the program design, and the verbs become the operations. Using this rule on the problem "Sort a list of integers," the program design should include a "list of integers" object type that has a "sort" operation. The Intlist program more closely matches the "natural" solution suggested by the problem description, whereas the second program invents a specialized type not clearly necessary for the solution.

A sorted list type might be just the type for different problems, especially as a specialized case of a list. For example, in a program that does a wide variety of list processing, a sorted list type might be useful to optimize searching or merging of lists. A compressed list type, representing lists with no duplicate elements, could also be part of a good list processing program.

This brings out another aspect of object-oriented design, the use of inheritance to create specialized versions of the basic object types. Rather than create an entirely different object type for each application, one builds new types from general base types. In our hypothetical list processing program, we would use `List` as our base class and have `Sortedlist` and `Compressedlist` as classes derived from `List`. The `sort` operation could be declared as a virtual function in the base class. The version of `sort` in `Sortedlist` would do nothing. No special version of `sort` would be needed for `Compressedlist`.

A guideline for recognizing when inheritance might be used for type specialization in an object-oriented design is to look for adjectives in the programming problem description. For the list processing problem, "sorted list" and "compressed list" indicate when derived types could be used. In the symbol table example of Chapter 5,"function table", "global table", and "class table" were eventually represented as classes derived from "table".

A problem description does not always conveniently identify the best object types with which to implement a program. Finding an abstraction common to a number of objects so that they can share one base type implementation is not necessarily a straightforward task. Designing a program is often a trial and error process, requiring several attempts at a precise problem description, identification of abstractions, and prototype implementations. This is not new or peculiar to object-oriented design.

What is new in object-oriented programming is the way of thinking of programs as implementations of object types instead of as implementations of algorithms. This conceptual shift is sometimes hard for a programmer to make. Abstract concepts and entities that are not tangible things may be particularly hard to recognize as candidates for object types.

It is not difficult to conceive of object types that correspond to real-world physical objects with which we are familiar. For example, devices like disk and tape drives are physical objects. Devices are one of the objects in the domain of an operating system kernel. In Chapter 5, we presented a class to serve as a generic interface to device drivers.

```
class Device {
  public:
    virtual int open(char *, int, int);
    virtual int close(int);
    virtual int read(int, char *, unsigned);
    virtual int write(int, char *, unsigned);
    virtual int ioctl(int, int ...);
    Device();
    ~Device();
};
```

This class can also be thought of as the base object type for all varieties of devices in an object-oriented design of an operating system. Using inheritance, variations of the type can be created to represent disk devices and tape devices.

```
class Disk : public Device {
  public:
    int open(char *, int, int);
    int close(int);
    int read(int, char *, unsigned);
    int write(int, char *, unsigned);
    int ioctl(int, int ...);
    Disk();
    ~Disk();
};
```

```
class Tape: public Device {
  public:
    // etc.
};
```

Although there are a variety of different device types, the kernel's view is of a number of identical device objects.

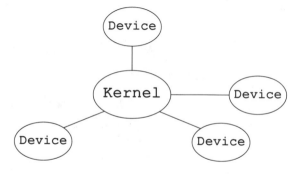

Many programs never deal directly with intuitively understandable representations of physical objects. The object types needed in these cases are part of an abstract problem domain. In an operating system, a process could be an object, even though "process" is conceived of as an activity.

A typical operating system kernel might represent a process by scattered data structures and functions that manipulate the various structures. In an object-oriented design, these data structures and functions are packed together in a class to create a process object type. The interface to the object type is the set of functions by which the kernel controls processes. In our example below, `class Proc` provides functions to put a process to sleep waiting for a certain event at a certain priority, to wake up a sleeping process, to save and restore the state of a running process, and to send a message, in the form of a message number, to the process. A constructor is provided so that a new `Proc` can be created from another, as when processes are forked. The destructor removes a terminated process from the system. Operations for swapping a processes in and out of the system are not provided in the example interface because these are considered part of the memory management of the hidden elements of the `Proc` object.

```
class Proc {
  public:
      int sleep( Sleepq *, int  );
      void wakeup();
      int save_runstate();
      void resume_runstate();
      int send_msg( int );
      Proc( Proc & );
      ~Proc();
};
```

Process objects can now be added to the kernel's view of its domain:

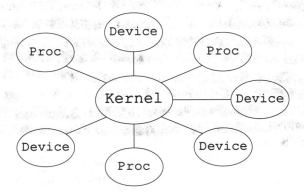

Another aspect of object-oriented design is recognizing a generic type. Again in the list processing program, there might be "lists of integers", "lists of strings", and "lists of employee records". All these lists of different element types could be built as instantiations of a generic list type. A clue for recognizing a generic type is that it is a container for other types. It is probably not worthwhile building a generic type, however, unless a program uses more than one instance of the type, or the type is to be reused in other programs.

It takes some practice for a programmer who is used to decomposing a design into functions to get used to designing in objects. Once a programmer catches on to the object-oriented way of thinking, however, she or he should be careful not to overdo it. As in the earlier example that creates a sorted list instead of sorting a list, it is usually possible to invent an object type to satisfy any purpose. The proliferation of concocted object types obscures the design of the program. A good object-oriented design clearly corresponds to the problem that the program is to solve, making the program easy to understand, implement, and maintain.

6.2 Object Types as Modules

In object-oriented programming, the elements of a problem correspond to design elements that are the object types that form the program modules. One advantage of this method of building programs is that there is a conceptual continuity across all phases of program construction, and the resulting object type modules can be easily reused.

The conceptual structure of a program not only remains the same from problem description through implementation, but also remains the same during refinement of a design. Once the object types are identified, the design is refined by adding details to these types. This contrasts with top-down stepwise refinement of a function, in which the higher level design is decomposed into a different structure. Having a complete design structure before all details are known aids rapid prototyping. Prototype implementations of object types can be achieved by putting in a few operations and hiding unfinished details, allowing the feasibility of a design to be tested early. Being able to put build prototypes quickly reduces the cost of trial-and-error design.

Consider a word processing program that manipulates strings. Once need for a string object type is identified in the program design, a `class` `String` can be quickly implemented by using simple data structures and existing library routines, like our first example of class String in Chapter 3. This simple version of String can be used in prototyping to identify exactly what string operations are needed. Adding operations to the prototype class String parallels the refinement of details in the program design. Once the feasibility of a design is proved, a more sophisticated implementation of String, like the one in Chapter 4, can replace the prototype version.

Because object-oriented design is not top down, the resulting program modules are more independent and therefore easier to reuse. A module is not incorporated into the design hierarchy of a particular program and so does not depend on a particular program structure. The object type module is an implementation of an element in a particular problem domain instead of a subfunction of one solution to a problem. The module can therefore be used for any program in the same or an overlapping problem domain. For example, String can be reused in any program that needs a type to represent words or text.

Another aspect of module reuse is the easy extensibility of object types by inheritance. The original module remains untouched as new functionality is added in a derived type. Modules that are general object types can easily be reused for many variations of a problem. The specialized type Pathname that was derived from String in Chapter 5 is an example of how a general type can be adapted for a specific purpose with inheritance.

6.3 Dynamic Object-Oriented Style

Object-oriented programming is associated with a programming style consisting of runtime creation of objects and dynamic binding of operations on objects. This style of programming originated with interpreted object-oriented languages and systems like Flavors and Smalltalk. These systems were designed for runtime flexibility and have proved to be successful tools for prototyping, immediate problem solving, and simulation.

It is possible to write object-oriented programs in C++ that consist entirely of runtime creation of object instances and that have dynamic binding of operations on objects with virtual functions. The creation of objects and invocation of object operations is done from within the text of a program that is compiled. Although the virtual function calls are dynamically bound, they are statically type checked. What C++ doesn't have in interactive flexibility, it makes up for in strong compile-time type checking and efficient execution.

Dynamic object-oriented programming is often used for simulations.

Object types are implemented to simulate different entities in the problem. Object instances are then set in motion to enact the simulation. The objects interact by invoking operations on one another and by creating new objects that enter the simulation. The rest of this chapter presents a program simulating airplane traffic at an airport.

The C++ task library is used in the airport simulation to allow different actions to run as coroutines. The coroutines in the simulation are the constructors of class `task` objects, or classes derived from `task`. The task library implements nonpreemptive scheduling, so each task must give up control on its own to give other tasks a chance to run. In this simulation, task execution is controlled by the `task` member function

```
        void task::delay( int )
```

which suspends the execution of the task for a given number of simulated time units. A library global variable, `clock`, keeps track of the passage of time. The function

```
        void task::cancel( int )
```

terminates the execution of the task.

The library also provides classes for implementing queues. The class types `qhead` and `qtail` are separate in the task library because they need to be able to function independently for the different tasks that put objects on and take objects off queues. The queue functions we use are

```
        qtail *qhead::tail()
```

for getting the `qtail` which is coupled with a particular `qhead`,

```
        int qtail::put( object * )
```

which adds an object to the end of the queue, and,

```
        object *qhead::get()
```

which removes an object from the head of a queue. Functions to check if a queue is full or empty are

```
        int qtail::rdspace()
```

which returns the amount of spaces left for adding more objects to the queue and

```
        int qhead::rdcount()
```

which gives the number of objects already on the queue. The class type object is the base type from which all queue elements must be derived. Because task and other classes in the task library have object as their root base type, objects of these types can be placed on queues.

The task library also provides random number generators. We use class urand to provide random numbers uniformly distributed over a given range, through the function

```
int urand::draw()
```

The main function creates an Airport task object, lets it run for a period of simulated time, then closes down the simulation and returns. As soon as the Airport is created main itself becomes a task running as a coroutine with the other tasks. The task system pointer thistask is needed to control the execution of main as a coroutine.

```
#include "Airport.h"

main() {
    Airport *ap = new Airport;
    thistask->delay( 5000 );
    delete ap;
    thistask->resultis(0);
}
```

The airport header file itself includes the header of the task library. The object types for the simulation are built from the task library types.

```
/* This is Airport.h */
#include "task.h"

class Plane : object {
    static int fltcount;
    long start;
    int fltno;
public:
    Plane() { fltno = ++fltcount; }
    long howlong() { return clock - start; }
    void set() { start = clock; }
    int flt() { return fltno; }
};

class PlaneQ {
    qhead *head;
    qtail *tail;
public:
    PlaneQ() {  head = new qhead( ZMODE, 50 );
                tail = head->tail();}
    void put( Plane *p ) { p->set();
                tail->put( (object*)p );}
    Plane *get() { return (Plane *)head->get(); }
    int isroom() { return tail->rdspace(); }
    int notempty() { return head->rdcount(); }
};

class AirControl : public task  {
    PlaneQ  *landing, *inair;
public:
    AirControl( PlaneQ *, PlaneQ * );
};
class GroundControl : public task {
    PlaneQ *takingoff, *onground;
public:
    GroundControl( PlaneQ*, PlaneQ* );
};

class Airport : public task {
    PlaneQ  *takingoff, *landing, *inair, *onground;
    AirControl *acontrol;
    GroundControl *gcontrol;
public:
    Airport();
    ~Airport();
};
```

The different object types are `Plane`, for airplanes, `PlaneQ`, for queues of airplanes waiting to use the airport facilities, `AirControl`, for directing airplanes in the air around the airport, `GroundControl`, for directing airplanes on the ground, and `Airport`, which consists of airplane queues and controllers for directing air and ground traffic. The `Airport` itself handles the control of the runway.

A `Plane` is derived from `object`, the base type that is manipulated by the task system. The implementation of `Plane` keeps track of flight time and delay information using the task library variable `clock`, which measures simulated time.

`PlaneQ` encapsulates a `qhead` and `qtail`, which implement a queue for holding planes. A `PlaneQ` is set up so that it holds fifty planes and so that a `get` an empty queue returns a null pointer. (Queues can also be created so that a `get` on an empty queue suspends the calling task.)

`AirControl`, `GroundControl`, and `Airport` are all `tasks`. When instances of these types are created, their constructors run as coroutines.

The `Airport` constructor creates the plane queues on which planes await service, and then the control tasks that feed the queues. It then goes into an infinite loop that runs until the `Airport` task is canceled. The airport serves one plane for landing and one plane for take off every ten simulated time units. If there are not already planes waiting, the planes are taken off the queues. Reports on the progress of a plane are made using `printf`. The reality of planes running out of fuel while waiting for landing is inelegantly simulated by a crash landing, which removes the plane from the simulation.

```cpp
Airport::Airport() {

    takingoff = new PlaneQ;
    inair = new PlaneQ;
    landing = new PlaneQ;
    onground = new PlaneQ;

    acontrol = new AirControl( landing, inair );
    gcontrol = new GroundControl( takingoff, onground);

    Plane *tp=0, *lp=0; // waiting planes
    int maxwait = 30;

    for(;;){
        delay( 10 );
        if( !lp ) lp = landing->get();
        if( !tp ) tp = takingoff->get();
        if( lp ){
            if( onground->isroom() ) {
                printf( "flight %d landing \n",
                    lp->flt());
                onground->put( lp );
                lp = 0;
            }
            else if( lp->howlong() > maxwait ) {
                printf( "flight %d crash landing!\n",
                    lp->flt());
                delete lp;
                lp = 0;
            } else
                printf( "flight %d landing delayed \n",
                    lp->flt());
        }
        if( tp ) {
            if( inair->isroom() ) {
                printf( "flight %d taking off\n",
                    tp->flt());
                inair->put( tp );
                tp = 0;
            } else
                printf( "flight %d take off delayed \n",
                    lp ->flt());
        }
    }
}
```

The `Airport` destructor cancels the `AirControl` task so that no more planes are scheduled for landing. It delays until all waiting planes have landed, and then cancels the remaining tasks running the airport.

```
Airport::~Airport() {
    acontrol->cancel(0);
    while( landing->notempty() )
        thistask->delay( 10 );
    gcontrol->cancel(0);
    printf("Airport Closed\n");
    cancel(0);
}
```

The `AirControl` schedules arriving planes for landing every one to thirty time units. The varying arrival time interval is implemented using `urand`, a random number generator type provided in the task library. In this case in which only a single airport is simulated, planes are created to be put on the landing queue or recycled from planes that have taken off from the airport.

```
AirControl:: AirControl( PlaneQ *landing,
                PlaneQ *inair ) {

    urand n( 1, 30 );

    for(;;){
        delay( n.draw() );

        Plane *p = inair->get();
        if( !p ) {
            p = new Plane;
        }
        if( landing->isroom() ) {
            printf ("flight %d arriving for landing\n",
                p->flt() );
            landing->put( p );
        } else {
            printf ("flight %d redirected\n",
                p->flt() );
            delete p;
        }
    }
}
```

The `GroundControl` takes ten to thirty time units to service a plane on the ground, and then schedules it for take off.

```
GroundControl::GroundControl( PlaneQ *takingoff,
                   PlaneQ *onground ) {

    urand n( 10, 30 );
    Plane *p = 0;

    for(;;){
        delay( n.draw() );
        if( !p ) p = onground->get();
        if( p ) {
            if( takingoff->isroom() ) {
                printf ("flight %d leaving gate\n",
                        p->flt() );
                takingoff->put( p );
                p = 0;
            } else
                printf ("flight %d delayed at gate\n",
                        p->flt() );
        }
    }
}
```

Here is the end of the output of the airport simulation:

```
flight 5 arriving for landing
flight 82 crash landing!
flight 84 arriving for landing
flight 9 landing delayed
flight 48 leaving gate
flight 9 landing
flight 48 taking off
flight 48 arriving for landing
flight 17 leaving gate
flight 83 landing
flight 17 taking off
flight 17 arriving for landing
flight 5 crash landing!
flight 84 crash landing!
flight 32 leaving gate
flight 48 landing
flight 32 taking off
flight 17 crash landing!
flight 60 leaving gate
Airport Closed
```

Frequent crash landings occurred in the simulation. This seems not to be caused by a backlog of landing plans, but by the short delay tolerance and a ground queue backlog. Different values can be tried for the maximum landing delay, ground service waits, arrival interval, and queue sizes to see the effects on the occurrence of crashes, delays, and redirected flights.

6.4   Exercises

Exercise 6-1. Add better handling of emergency landings to the airport simulation. □

Exercise 6-2. Implement the `Intlist` abstract data type used in the example in the first section of this chapter. Implement the `Sortedintlist` type as a type derived from `Intlist`. □

Exercise 6-3. Redesign the air and ground control modules in the airport simulation to be specialized versions of a control type. □

Exercise 6-4. †Extend the airport simulation to include a national flight control that routes flights among different airports. □

Exercise 6-5. Many applications are conceptualized as moving from an initial state through a sequence of states in response to input. At each state, some action is performed. Automated banking programs, airline reservation systems, and compiler lexical analyzers can be conceptualized in this way, for example. Typically, the state transitions are encoded in a table indexed by the current state and an integer code corresponding to the input. For each new state, the action corresponding to that state is performed.

What are the advantages and potential problems of this approach?

An alternative framing of this conceptualization is to create a state object that encapsulates all the semantics for a given state, including next state and action to be performed.

What are the advantages of the object-oriented approach in this situation? What are the disadvantages?

Design an automated banking application and implement it using both approaches. □

CHAPTER 7: **Storage Management**

In programming texts, the topic of storage management is often considered unimportant or an area that is handled by the language or operating system. Proper control of storage management is essential to the correctness of an application, however, and can be important to its efficiency.

Inefficient allocation and freeing of memory can contribute greatly to the inefficiency of an application by causing too many system calls to get more memory, by fragmenting available storage and causing "thrashing" as pages are continually swapped in and out of memory, or—in certain hardware environments—by running out of memory entirely. Ad hoc attempts to address these inefficiencies can lead to incorrect storage management, such as premature freeing or accidental aliasing of a block of memory.

Storage management needs are application specific. In some cases, all storage management needs are statically determined, in others they are almost entirely dynamic. Frequently, there is application-specific information that one can take advantage of to produce an efficient storage management scheme. Although C++ provides default general storage management, it also provides the ability to customize storage management for a given problem area, class type, or application.

7.1 Storage Management in Constructors and Destructors

We have seen constructors as allocators of new objects, as initializers of already existing objects, and as one kind of user-defined conversion. These are simply three different views of the same operation, creating an object of a given type from a sequence of values.

Unlike member functions, constructors have a hidden mechanism that is not explicitly coded by the programmer. We've already described some of this, such as automatic initialization of base classes and members that have constructors that can be invoked without arguments. Let us look in detail at some constructors, and see what goes on behind the scenes.

```
complex::complex( double r = 0.0, double i = 0.0 ) {
    re = r;
    im = i;
}
```

The constructor for class `complex` is straightforward. First it ensures that there is storage for the complex number, and then it executes the body of the constructor (provided by the programmer) to initialize the storage. Every constructor starts with some implicitly inserted code that checks the value of `this` to determine whether or not there is an object to work with. If `this` is null there is no object to work with, and the constructor calls `operator new` to get the storage for the object.

Two cases in which the implicit `this` argument is non-null are for static and automatic objects. A static object (whether its linkage is `static` or `extern`, see Chapter 2) is always in existence. An automatic object has its storage allocated automatically on entrance to the function in which it is defined.

```
complex zero;   // static (linkage extern)
complex zilch() {
    complex a( 1, 2 );  // auto
    return a * zero;
}
```

The storage for `zero` is always around, and the storage for `a` is allocated on entry to `zilch`. In neither case is `operator new` called in `complex::complex`. But in code like

```
complex *cp = new complex;
```

the value of `this` is null on entry to `complex::complex`, and `operator new` is called.

Another case in which `this` is non-null on entry to a constructor is for base class and member initializations, because the storage for these will have already been allocated by the derived or containing class constructor. For example, when we allocate one of the derived abstract syntax tree node types of Chapter 5, we invoke the derived class constructor, which allocates storage (if necessary) and invokes the base class constructor. The code

```
Node *np = new Int(5);
```

invokes the constructor for class `Int` with a null `this` value.

```
Int::Int( int v ) {
    value = v;
}
```

First the constructor allocates storage for the `Int` object by calling `operator new` and assigning the returned address to `this`. Then the base class constructor `Node::Node` is invoked implicitly. Because `this` is non-null in the call of the base class constructor, `operator new` is not called in `Node::Node`.

The same result occurs in a multilevel class hierarchy. When we say

```
extern Node *x, *y;
Node *np = new Plus( x, y );
```

we invoke

```
Plus::Plus( Node *l, Node *r )
    : Binop(l,r) {}
```

which allocates storage for the `Plus` object and explicitly invokes the base class constructor, `Binop::Binop`, with the initialized `this` pointer as well as pointers to the left and right subtrees. The `Binop` constructor implicitly invokes the `Node` constructor. Because the storage for the `Plus` object has already been allocated (including that for the `Node` and `Binop` parts of a `Plus`) neither the `Node` nor the `Binop` constructors call `operator new`.

Like constructors, destructors have hidden mechanism to invoke member and base class destructors and `operator delete` to deallocate storage. In the same way that a constructor for a class allocates the storage for its member and base class parts, the destructor for a class deallocates the storage for its members and bases as well. Recall the unary minus node type from the node hierarchy of Chapter 5.

```
class Uminus : public Node {
    Node *operand;
  public:
    Uminus( Node *o ) { operand = o; }
    ~Uminus() { delete operand; }
    // ...
};
```

The `Uminus` constructor first allocates storage, then invokes the base class `Node` constructor. On return from the base class constructor, it executes its body, initializing `operand`. The destructor performs essentially the reverse sequence. First, it executes its body, deleting `operand` (by explicitly invoking its destructor), then invokes the base class `Node` destructor. On return from the base class destructor, `Uminus::~Uminus` calls `operator delete` to deallocate the storage for the class. Similarly to calls to `operator new` in constructors, `operator delete` is not called by the base class or member destructors, or if the object being destroyed is static or auto. The sequence of base class and member destructor calls, and the call to `operator delete` are inserted before each `return` in the body of the destructor, including the implicit `return` at the end of the destructor's function block.

7.2 Operator New and Operator Delete

Operators `new` and `delete` are predefined library functions that manage free store or "heap" memory.

```
extern void *operator new( long );
extern void operator delete( void * );
```

Note that `operator new` returns a block of free store of at least the number of bytes specified in its argument, and `operator delete` frees a block of free store previously allocated by `operator new`. In addition, `operator new` returns a null pointer if it fails to allocate the requested storage.

```
f() {
    int *ip = new int[1000000];
    if( !ip ) {
        error( "ran out of memory!" );
        exit( 1 );
    }
}
```

To give more control over memory allocation, an extern pointer, `_new_handler`, can be set to a function to be called if `operator new` fails. Until either it is able to allocate the requested memory or `_new_handler` is null, `operator new` will iteratively call the function referred to by `_new_handler`.

```
extern void (*_new_handler)();

void
give_up() {
    error( "ran out of memory!" );
    exit( 1 );
}

void
increase_limit() {
    // Ask OS for more space.
    extern long ulimit( int, long );
    ulimit( 3, 0 );
    _new_handler = give_up;
}

f() {
    _new_handler = increase_limit;
    int *ip = new int[1000000];
}
```

Now if operator new fails to allocate the requested amount of memory, it will call increase_limit (indirectly through _new_handler) to increase the amount of space available to the program. If it still fails, or if subsequent calls to operator new fail, give_up prints a message and terminates the program.

This is a very flexible mechanism, and the "standard" library operators new and delete serve for most applications. We can also override the standard versions, however, by supplying our own versions of operator new and operator delete. These user-defined versions are used in place of the standard versions.

For example, operator new does not guarantee that the storage it returns is initialized to all zeros, so we might want to supply versions of new and delete that guarantee zeroed storage.

```
extern void *
operator new( long sz ) {
    // calloc returns zeroed storage
    extern char *calloc(unsigned, unsigned);
    return calloc( 1, sz );
}
```

```
extern void
operator delete( void *p ) {
    extern void free( char * );
    free( (char *)p );
}
```

Note that setting _new_handler will no longer have any effect on the behavior of operator new (unless we explicitly code it). _new_handler is simply part of the implementation of the standard library operator new.

We can be more ambitious in our replacement of the standard memory management routines. For instance, if our applications perform many allocations of small amounts of memory, and rarely free memory once it has been allocated, we can design an efficient memory management scheme that takes this pattern of usage into account.

```
extern void (*_new_handler)() = 0;

extern void *
operator new( long nbytes ) {
    extern char *calloc( unsigned, unsigned );
    static const long BSIZ = 4 * 1024;
    static char ibuf[BSIZ];
    static char *start = ibuf;
    static char *end = ibuf + BSIZ;
    static const long ALIGN = sizeof( double );

    if( nbytes & (ALIGN-1) )
        nbytes += ALIGN - nbytes % ALIGN;

    if( end - start < nbytes ) {
        long bufsiz = BSIZ > nbytes ? BSIZ : nbytes;
        while( !(start = calloc( 1, bufsiz )) )
            if( _new_handler )
                _new_handler();
            else
                return 0;
        end = start + bufsiz;
    }
    start += nbytes;
    return start - nbytes;
}
```

This version of operator new first rounds up the memory request to ensure alignment (of the following request), then checks that there is enough unallocated space in the current buffer to fulfill the request. For convenience, two pointers indicate the first free location in the current buffer and the end of the buffer. If there is enough space in the current buffer to handle the request, the pointer indicating the next free location is updated, and the address of the allocated storage is returned.

If there is not enough space in the current buffer to satisfy the request, then a new buffer, large enough to handle the request but of at least a minimum size, is requested of the operating system. If the request for a new buffer fails, the standard `_new_handler` mechanism is implemented to give the user the ability to make some sort of recovery.

By requesting infrequent, large blocks of memory from the operating system, this version of `operator new` should perform better than the standard version for applications that issue frequent requests for small amounts of storage. Because the initial buffer is allocated statically, no requests may be made to operating system at all.

Because our applications rarely free memory, deletions can be ignored. Because it does nothing at all, `operator delete` is most efficiently implemented as an inline function.

```
inline void
operator delete( void * ) {}
```

An important aspect of our versions of `operator new` and `operator delete` is that they have the same user interface as the standard `new` and `delete`. Some of this is required: `operator new` must be of type `void *(long)`, and `operator delete` must be of type `void (void *)`. We also retained the same error condition in `operator new` of returning null on failure, however. We can then encapsulate these routines in a file to prevent users from taking advantage of implementation-specific knowledge. Maintaining a standard interface and hiding the implementation details gives the same advantages as an abstract data type (in fact, it *is* an abstract data type), and we can change the implementation of memory management without affecting user code.

7.3 Storage Management of Arrays

The standard C++ library also defines two functions that manage storage for arrays of class objects, `_vec_new` and `_vec_delete`.

```
void *_vec_new( void *, int, int, void * );
void _vec_delete( void *, int, int, void *, int );
```

These functions are not used for all array allocations and deallocations, but only those whose elements require constructor initialization or destruction. Thus

```
int *ip = new int[3][4][5];
```

results in a call to `operator new` requesting space for 60 `int`s, and

```
struct Pair {
    void *first, *second;
};
Pair *list = new Pair[12];
```

results in a request for space sufficient for 12 `Pair`s. If the members of the array require a constructor initialization, however,

```
struct Pair2 {
    void *first, *second;
    Pair2() { first = second = 0; }
};
Pair2 *list2 = new Pair2[12];
```

then `_vec_new` is invoked to first allocate space for the array, then invoke the constructor for each element.

In a similar way, `_vec_delete` is invoked if an array whose element type has a destructor is deleted. In this case, however, it is necessary to supply explicitly the size of the array.

```
struct Strlist {
    Strlist *next;
    String str;
    Strlist();
    ~Strlist();
};
Strlist *slist = new Strlist[100];  // call _vec_new
delete [100] slist; // call _vec_delete
```

If the size information were missing, the compiler would generate a call to `operator delete` to delete a single `Strlist`. In the case of deletions that do not result in a call of `_vec_delete`, the explicit size information is ignored.

```
int *ip = new int[1000000];
delete [10] ip; // size info ignored, fortunately...
delete [12] list2;  // size info ignored
```

As with `operator new` and `operator delete`, we can supply our own versions of `_vec_new` and `_vec_delete`. The arguments to `_vec_new` are, in sequence, the address of the array being "allocated," the number of elements in the array, the size (in bytes) of an array element, and the address of the initializing constructor. The first argument is used in a way similar to `this` in a constructor, as `_vec_new` and `_vec_delete` are also used to initialize and destroy static and automatic arrays.

```
static Strlist hashtab[512];
```

The first argument to `_vec_new` is the address of the array for statics and automatics, and zero otherwise. The arguments to `_vec_delete` are the same as those to `_vec_new`, except that there is an additional argument that flags whether or not the storage is to be released. For static and automatic arrays, the flag is zero and the storage is not released; otherwise the flag is one, and the storage is released.

The interface to `_vec_new` shows a severe limitation on its use. Because the only information provided to `_vec_new` is the address of the constructor, it is not possible to invoke `_vec_new` with a constructor that takes arguments (even default arguments). In current implementations of C++ it is also illegal to cause `_vec_new` to be invoked with a constructor for a class with virtual base classes.

```
complex cary[10];    // error!
Monitored_network_device boards[3]; // error!
```

In the first declaration, the implicit constructor initialization makes use of default arguments. In the second declaration, some base classes are virtual. Because the range of legal initializers for arrays of class objects is so limited, it is generally good advice to avoid arrays of all but the most simple class types.

7.4 Class-Specific New and Delete

The implementations of `new` and `delete` we've seen so far have been general-purpose. Like the standard library versions, they are meant to serve for all types in all cases. As we observed earlier, however, type or application-specific knowledge can be employed to speed up memory management significantly. To take advantage of specialized knowledge, C++ provides the ability to define class-specific versions of `operator new` and `operator delete`.

For example, class `complex` has a very small and simple implementation, and in addition does not require zeroed memory. We can speed up memory management significantly with class-specific `new` and `delete` operators that take advantage of the implementation-specific details.

```
class complex {
    double re, im;
  public:
    void *operator new( long );
    void operator delete( void * );
    // ...
};
```

These operators are invoked whenever an object of type `complex` is allocated or deleted, whether or not the allocation or deletion is performed in the scope of class `complex`.

```
#include <complex.h>

main() {
    complex *cp = new complex( 12 );
    int *ip = new int;
    *ip = 12;
    complex cgross = *cp * *ip;
}
```

Note that `cp` refers to storage allocated by `complex::operator new`, and `ip` refers to storage allocated by `::operator new`. In addition, `cgross` is an automatic and did not require a call to any `operator new` for its initialization.

We implement storage management for `complex` by allocating elements of a static array. Freed elements are maintained on a freelist. The implementation of `complex::operator new` first checks the freelist for a previously allocated and freed element. If there are none, but there are elements of the array that have not yet been allocated, one is allocated. Otherwise `operator new` fails and returns null.

```
static const int MAX = 100;

static class rep {
    static rep *free;
    static int num_used;
    union {
    double store[2];
    rep *next;
    };
    friend complex;
} mem[MAX];
```

```
void *
complex::operator new( long ) {
    if( rep::free ) {
        rep *tmp = rep::free;
        rep::free = rep::free->next;
        return tmp->store;
    }
    else if( rep::num_used < MAX )
        return mem[ rep::num_used++ ].store;
    else
        return 0;
}
```

The implementation of `complex::operator delete` just adds the element of the array being freed to the head of the freelist.

```
void
complex::operator delete( void *p ) {
    ((rep *)p)->next = rep::free;
    rep::free = (rep *)p;
}
```

Note that `complex::operator new` does not even check the value of the argument but always returns storage large enough to hold an object of type `complex`. The implicit assumption is that no class will be derived from class `complex`. This may be a good assumption, but, if it were not the case, we could be in trouble.

```
class point3 : public complex {
    // a point in 3-space
    double z;
  public:
    // ...
};
point3 *p = new point3;
```

Because `point3` inherits `new` and `delete` along with the other members of class `complex`, the constructor call for `point3` invokes `complex::operator new` and returns storage large enough for a `complex`, but not necessarily large enough for a `point3`.

We can go further in designing class-specific `new` and `delete` than considering just the properties of the type; we can also design a memory allocation scheme that depends on properties of the application as a whole.

Consider the calculator program for which we designed the node hierarchy of Chapter 5. Suppose our calculator program builds only a single abstract syntax tree at a time, evaluates it, and deletes the entire tree. Given this, we can redesign memory management to be much more efficient.

```
class Node {
  protected:
    Node() {}
    void *operator new( long );
    void operator delete( void * );
    // ...
};
```

`Node::operator new` (and `Node::operator delete`) are inherited by classes derived from `Node`, so we must either provide a different `operator new` for each derived class, or make `Node::operator new` sufficiently general to deal with all node types. Here we do the latter.

```
static const int SZ = 1000;

static struct buf {
    buf *next;
    char mem[SZ];
} b, *bp = &b;

static char *memp = b.mem;

void *
Node::operator new( long sz ) {
    if( memp+sz > &bp->mem[SZ] )
        if( bp->next ) {
            bp = bp->next;
            memp = bp->mem;
        }
        else if( bp = bp->next = new buf )
            memp = bp->mem;
        else
            return 0;
    char *r = memp;
    memp += sz;
    return r;
}
```

We start with a statically allocated buffer whose size we estimate will be sufficient for most runs of the application and allocate additional buffers from free store as needed.

Note that the use of `new` to allocate the overflow buffers refers to the global `operator new` because the buffer is not of type `Node` or a type derived from `Node`.

Note that `operator delete` takes advantage of the fact that any use of `delete` is to release the entire abstract syntax tree. We ignore the argument and reset the memory management pointers to their initial values. We hold on to any additional buffers we may have allocated in order to prevent their reallocation. We also get rid of the destructors in `Node` and in the classes derived from it, because they are superfluous.

```
void
Node::operator delete( void * ) {
    bp = &b;
    memp = b.mem;
}
```

This version of `new` and `delete` is much faster than the standard one, but it is also tightly coupled to the way we use abstract syntax trees in a specific application.

As in member functions it is possible, but rarely advisable, to assign to `this` in a constructor. In so doing, the programmer takes over the task of getting storage for a class object. If `this` is explicitly assigned to in the body of a constructor, then there is no implicit call to `operator new`, and all explicit and implicit base class and member initializations are repeated after each such assignment.

Assigning to `this` in a constructor is dangerous. Consider taking over storage allocation in the list node constructor of Chapters 4 and 5. For illustration, we've moved the member initializations from the body of the constructor to the member initialization list.

```
list::list( ETYPE e, list *lst ) : el(e), link(lst) {
    if( !this )
        this = my_alloc( sizeof( list ) );
}
```

This will not work for static or automatic objects. The initializations in the member initialization list are performed only after assignments to `this`, but no assignment is performed for static or automatic objects because the value of `this` is non-null on entry to the constructor.

Even if we expect no static or automatic `list` objects to be to be created, we'll still have problems because `list` could serve as a base class or as member in another class.

```
list2::list2( ETYPE e, list2 *fl, list2 *bl )
        : list(e,fl), link(bl) {}
```

There are at least two problems with this code. The first is that, because

the value of this is non-null for the base class initialization, list::el
and list::link will not be initialized. Second, the storage for a list2
object, including the list part of a list2, is supplied by
operator new, not my_alloc. Whether or not this is a problem is application dependent, but presumably we had reasons for supplying an alternate allocator for lists.

We can fix the first problem by supplying a seemingly unnecessary assignment to this in list::list to get the initializations no matter what
the value of this on entry.

```
if( this )
    this = this;    // static, auto, base or member
else
    this = my_alloc( sizeof( list ) );
```

This is not only unnatural and error prone, but it also causes the implicit initialization code to be inserted twice into the body of the constructor.

Similarly, one can gain control over deallocation in destructors by assigning to this. If the value of this is null before a return, then the
member and base class destructors are not invoked, and operator
delete is not called.

In general, class specific versions of operator new and operator
delete should be used in preference to assigning to this.

7.5 Operator ->

Storage management is concerned not only with allocation and freeing of
storage but also with accessing it. Applications frequently require code sequences that do some processing either before or after a storage access.

```
do something
access storage
do something else
```

Because these code sequences are not enforced in an automatic way, they
can be left out either inadvertently or as an "optimization."

```
class info {
    void f();
    // ...
};

info *p;      // ALWAYS check that p is non-null!!!

// ...

void
process_info() {
    // p is usually non-null...
    p->f();
    // ...
}
```

The clever optimization in `process_info` leads to disaster.

To help deal with problems of this sort, C++ allows the -> operator to be overloaded, giving the ability to create "smart" pointers that can encapsulate both checking and access semantics. Like operator () and operator [], operator -> must be a member function. It must be declared to take no argument and to return either a class type that has operator -> defined or a pointer to a class type.

Notice that, although the predefined -> operator is binary, user-defined operator -> is declared as unary. The idea is that a user-defined operator -> produces, either directly or indirectly, a pointer to an object of class type. This pointer is then used with the predefined > operator to access a member of that class.

```
class infoP {
    static info null_info;
    info *p;
  public:
    info *operator ->()
        { return p ? p : &null_info; }
    infoP( info *ip )
        { p = ip; }
    infoP &operator =( infoP ip )
        { return *this = ip; }
};
```

This is one solution to our previous problem; `infoP` is a smart pointer type that never returns a null pointer value to be used in a reference. In addition, it disallows any pointer operations, like ++, +, and so on, that could lead to a bad address.

```
infoP p;
// ...
void
process_info() {
    p->f(); // safe
    // ...
}
```

The access `p->f` first invokes `infoP::operator ->` on p, producing a value of type `info *`, which is then used to access the member `info::f`.

`operator ->` can also be declared to return a class type that defines an `operator ->`.

```
class infowarn {
    infoP &p;
  public:
    infowarn( infoP &ip ) : p(ip) {}
    infoP &operator ->() {
        warn( "accessing an info!" );
        return p;
    }
};
```

An `infowarn` object behaves like an `infoP` object on use, except that it prints a message before performing a safe access.

```
infowarn wp = p;
// ...
wp->f();
```

The access `wp->f` first invokes `infowarn::operator ->`, which prints a message and returns an `infoP`. Then `infoP::operator ->` is invoked, returning an `info *`, which is used to access `info::f`.

As a more realistic example of the use of smart pointers, suppose we have a file of records on disk, and we want to be able to write applications that use these records as if they were elements of an in-memory array, without being concerned with system-dependent functions of reading and writing disk records. Because there is a large number of records, however, we can't simply read them all into memory, and in any case relatively few records are examined by any given application, and fewer still are changed. We can't afford the overhead of reading and writing a large number of disk records.

We approach this problem by providing two types. The first represents a file of records, and the second is a smart pointer to a file record.

```
struct rec {      // a disk record
    int key;
    int value;
    // ...
};

class File {
    FILE *fp;
    sary *hd;
    rec *operator [](int);
  public:
    File(char *);
    ~File();
    friend Ptr;
};
```

A user creates a file object by supplying the path name of the file to be
opened. The FILE type and the routines for opening, closing, reading, and
writing files are system dependent. Here we use the stdio functions.

```
File::File( char *fname ) {
    fp = fopen( fname, "r+" );
    hd = 0;
}
```

Because we expect to read and write relatively few records, we implement
File as a sparse array. Our sparse array is an unordered linked list of index, record pairs.

```
class sary {
    sary *next;
    int index;
    rec *p;
    sary( int, sary *, FILE * );
    friend File;
};
```

Thus a File consists of a system-dependent file descriptor and a sparse
array of file records. File::operator [] creates elements of the
sparse array whenever there is an attempt to index an element that is not
present in the array.

```
rec *
File::operator [] ( int i ) {
    for( sary *sp = hd; sp; sp = sp->next )
        if( sp->index == i )
            break;
    if( !sp )
        sp = hd = new sary( i, hd, fp );
    return sp->p;
}
```

The sparse array node constructor creates the node and reads in the relevant record from disk. In addition it makes a copy of the record for later comparison. The disk record is not updated if it hasn't been changed.

```
sary::sary( int i, sary *n, FILE *fp ) {
    const int sz = sizeof( rec );
    index = i;
    next = n;
    p = (rec *) new char[2*sz];
    fseek( fp, i*sz, 0 );
    fread( (char *)p, sz, 1, fp );
    *(p+1) = *p;
}
```

The destructor for `File` updates to disk those records that have changed, deletes the sparse array, and closes the file.

```
File::~File() {
    const int sz = sizeof(rec);
    sary *sp = hd;
    while( hd ) {
        if( memcmp(sp->p[0], sp->p[1], sz) != 0 ) {
            fseek( fp, sp->index*sz, 0 );
            fwrite( (char *)sp->p, sz, 1, fp );
        }
        hd = hd->next;
        delete sp;
    }
    fclose( fp );
}
```

The main user interface to the `File` of database records is through a smart pointer type.

```
class Ptr {
    int index;
    File *fp;
  public:
    rec *operator->();
    rec &operator[](int);
    rec &operator *();
    Ptr( File *f, int i = 0 ) : fp(f), index(i) {}
    friend Ptr operator +(Ptr, int);
    friend Ptr operator +(int, Ptr);
    friend int operator -(Ptr, Ptr);
    friend Ptr operator -(Ptr, int);
    Ptr &operator ++();
    Ptr &operator --();
    Ptr &operator +=(int);
    Ptr &operator -=(int);

    friend int operator ==(Ptr, Ptr);
    friend int operator !=(Ptr, Ptr);
    friend int operator <(Ptr, Ptr);
    friend int operator <=(Ptr, Ptr);
    friend int operator >(Ptr, Ptr);
    friend int operator >=(Ptr, Ptr);
};
```

A `Ptr` is implemented as a pointer to a `File` and, considering the `File` to be an array of records, a current index into the `File`. We provide all the usual operations for pointer arithmetic.

```
Ptr &
Ptr::operator ++() {
    index++;
    return *this;
}

int
operator ==( Ptr a, Ptr b ) {
    return a.index == b.index;
}
```

The implementations of the other operators are similar. The arithmetic pointer operations are performed on the index of the file record, and no reference is made to the underlying `File` until necessary.

The actual work of a reference is done by `File::operator []`, and our smart pointer just returns the `File` array element corresponding to `Ptr::index`.

```
rec *
Ptr::operator ->() {
    return (*fp)[index];
}
```

For the predefined pointer types in C++ there is a correspondence between the operators ->, *, and [], such that p->m is equivalent to (*p).m, and *(p+i) is equivalent to p[i]. As with other equivalences that exist in the predefined parts of the language, such as that between ++ and += 1, if we want similar equivalences to hold for our user-defined operations, they must be defined explicitly.

```
rec &
Ptr::operator *() {
    return *(*fp)[index];
}

rec &
Ptr::operator [](  int i ) {
    return *(*fp)[index+i];
}
```

Now we can write applications. Suppose we have an ordered array of database records on disk, and we want to find and alter the value of one record.

```
void
alter( int key, char *file, int num_recs, int val ) {
    File f = file;
    Ptr mid = f;
    Ptr low(f,0), high(f,num_recs-1);
    while( low <= high ) {
        mid = low + (high-low)/2;
        if( mid->key < key )
            high = mid - 1;
        else if( mid->key > key )
            low = mid + 1;
        else {
            mid->value = val;
            break;
        }
    }
}
```

Note that alter opens a file and creates a sparse array of file records with the declaration of f, and creates three smart pointers into f, low, mid, and high, which are used to do a binary search on the file records. If the record corresponding to the argument `key` is found, its value is altered. The destructor for `f` is activated before the return to clean up the sparse array of file records and update the disk record of the changed element.

7.6   X(X&)

A constructor that can be invoked with an argument of its own class's type specifies how to initialize an object of that class with another object of that class. Because such a constructor is usually written as taking a single argument of type reference to the class of which it is a member, this concept is abbreviated as `X(X&)` (pronounced ''X of X ref'').

We have already seen uses of `X(X&)`. The `String` type of Chapter 4 uses a `String(String&)` constructor and a member `operator =(String&)` to ensure that whenever a `String` is copied (in an initialization and an assignment, respectively) the correct reference counts are maintained in the underlying `String_rep` objects. Defining an `X(X&)` constructor for a class states that the operation of copying objects of that class type must be carefully controlled.

As we saw in Chapter 3, initializations occur not only as part of a declaration or in constructor member initialization lists, but also in two other contexts: initialization of function formal arguments with actual arguments, and initialization of function return values with return expressions.

Consider initializing a formal argument with an actual argument. In some cases a constructor or conversion operator is invoked to convert the actual argument into a value of the correct type for the formal argument. In some cases it is necessary for the caller to create a temporary object in which to create the value before copying it onto the formal argument.

```
void f( complex );
f(12);
```

In converting the integer `12` into a `complex` value, a temporary `complex` object is created in the caller and initialized with the class `complex` constructor. The value of the temporary is copied onto the formal argument. Therefore the formal argument of `f` is initialized in the caller of `f`, and not in `f` itself. Here is another example using the abstract syntax tree node types of Chapter 5.

```
Int
incr( Int i ) {
    return i.eval() + 1;    // danger!
}
```

This code is problematic for a couple of reasons. First, because the type of the return expression, `int`, does not match the function return type, `Int`, the compiler creates a temporary `Int` object, initializes it with the `Int` constructor, and returns the value of the temporary object. Class `Int` also has a destructor (inherited from class `Node`), however, so the temporary `Int` object is destroyed before `incr` returns. In a similar way the formal argument `i` is destroyed before the return. If the call to `incr` generates a temporary object to initialize the formal argument, then that temporary object will also be destroyed in the caller.

```
extern int val;
Int x = incr( val );    // creates temp
```

Therefore, in handling the formal argument, there are two destructor calls and only a single constructor call: a constructor and destructor call for the temporary in the caller, and a destructor (only) for the formal argument in `incr`.

In fact, these are not problems for users of the abstract syntax tree hierarchy, because applications that use it do not use node types for arguments and returns, but rather use pointers and references to node types.

```
Int *
incr( Int &i ) {
    return new Int( i.eval() + 1 );
}
```

In this version of `incr`, no destructor is activated in the body of the function. These would be serious problems for users of the `String` class, however, because the unbalanced generation of constructor and destructor calls would invalidate the reference counts in the `String_rep` objects.

For this reason, class types that define an `X(X&)` constructor are treated differently from other types when used as formal argument and return types. If a class `X` defines `X(X&)`, then formal arguments of type `X` are treated as if they were of type `X&` for the purposes of initialization and destruction, but like `X` in all other contexts. Therefore, for `X` arguments, as for `X&` arguments, the actual storage for the formal argument is in the caller, and not in the called function.

Similarly, a function that is declared to return an `X` value actually initializes storage for an `X` object in the caller, rather than returning an `X` object.

In moving the storage for the formal arguments and return value to the caller, no destructors are activated for these objects in the called function, and a one-to-one correspondence between construction and destruction is maintained.

```
String
incr( String s ) {
    return s + "1";
}
```

No destructor is activated for the s formal parameter, and the return statement initializes storage in the caller. The caller both initializes and destroys the formal argument, and destroys the return value initialized by the return.

7.7 Implicit Copy Semantics

We've seen that it's necessary to define X(X&) and a member operator =(X&) to get control of copy semantics for objects of class X. (It is also possible to use a nonmember operator =(X&,X&), but this practice is discouraged for reasons including those given in the String example of Chapter 4.) Objects of class X can occur as members and base classes of other class types, however, and the same copy semantics must apply to these member and base class X objects as to X objects that are not embedded in another object.

```
class Text {
    Text *next;
    String phrase;
  public:
    Text( Text & );
    Text &operator =( Text & );
    // ...
};
```

Class Text defines copy semantics with an X(X&) constructor and a member assignment operator. These are implemented so as to preserve the copy semantics of the String member.

```
Text::Text( Text &t )
    : phrase( t.phrase ) {
    // ...
}

Text &
Text::operator =( Text &t ) {
    phrase = t.phrase;
    // ...
}
```

In both cases we explicitly supply the correct initialization or assignment of the `String` member.

Even if a class type does not explicitly define its copy semantics, non-default semantics are required if a member or base class does.

```
class Empl {
    long ssn;
    String name;
    // ...
};
```

To ensure that the correct copy semantics are performed in all cases, C++ implicitly defines them if necessary. If any member or base class of a class defines X(X&) or member operator =(X&), and there are no explicit copy semantics defined for the class, then they are defined implicitly by the compiler. For a class X they are (implicitly) declared as

```
X::X( const X & );
const X &X::operator =( const X & );
```

The semantics of each of these is to invoke the appropriate X(X&) or member operator =(X&) for each member and base that requires it, and simply copy the remaining class members.

Therefore the definition of class `Empl` includes implicit definitions of

```
Empl::Empl( const Empl & );
```

and

```
const Empl &Empl::operator =( const Empl & );
```

These ensure that the proper copy semantics are performed for the `String` member of `Empl`, and code involving copying of `Empl` objects does not affect the correctness of the `String` member, `name`.

```
extern Empl a;
Empl b = a; // Empl::Empl
a = b;   // Empl::operator=
```

7.8 Exercises

Exercise 7-1. Implement `operator new` and `operator delete` replacements for the standard versions that return zeroed storage and have the identical interface as the standard versions, including the definition and use of `_new_handler`. □

Exercise 7-2. †Implement the standard library versions of `_vec_new` and `_vec_delete`. □

Exercise 7-3. Explain why, in addition to its other faults, the first implementation of `sorted_collection` in Chapter 4 as a fixed-size array is not suitable as the basis for a generic type. (Hint: Consider instantiating the `sorted_collection` to hold a `complex` type.) □

Exercise 7-4. Generalize the implementation of operators `new` and `delete` for class `complex` so that they can handle storage requests of arbitrary size. □

Exercise 7-5. When using the application-specific versions of operators `new` and `delete` for class `Node`, how do the semantics of the following two functions differ?

```
void
limited1() {
    Node *np =
        new Plus (
            new Int( 1 ),
            new Int( 2 )
        );
    int result = np->eval();
    delete np;
    return result;
}
```

```
void
limited2() {
    Node *np =
        new Plus(
            new Int( 1 ),
            new Int( 2 )
        );
    int result = np->eval();
    Node *p;
    delete p;
    return result;
}
```

Is this behavior a fault or a feature of our implementation of operators new and delete? □

Exercise 7-6. In our implementation of complex::operator new there is an implicit dependency on the hidden representation of the complex type. What is it? Modify the implementation of complex::operator new to adjust itself automatically to changes in the hidden representation of class complex. □

Exercise 7-7. †Design a generic smart pointer type that is guaranteed to point only to free store (heap). □

CHAPTER 8: **Libraries**

Traditionally, a program library is a collection of functions, or functions and data structures that provide a specific functionality. For example, there are libraries of mathematical functions, access to operating system services, data structure descriptions of standard file formats, and standard input and output routines.

Libraries of this sort provide three important benefits. First, they provide general purpose code from a single source. Code reuse reduces the time required to design, code, and test applications and increases the likelihood that code is correct. Second, a standard library is also a standard interface. If machine- and environment-dependent aspects of an application are encapsulated within a library with a standard interface, the task of porting that application to different environments is greatly reduced. Third, a library developed in support of a particular application area reduces the difficulty of designing and coding applications in that area by hiding low-level details of the implementation and representing higher-level concepts in the library interface. For example, users of a standard I/O library need not be concerned with details of buffering and hardware devices, but can design and code using the higher-level concepts of "seek," "read," and "write."

In this chapter we discuss how the programming paradigms and supporting C++ language features described in previous chapters allow us to extend the traditional concept of a library to allow for greater code reuse, interface sharing, and conceptual support for design and coding.

8.1   Interface to Existing Libraries

As we discussed in Chapter 0, programming techniques and design paradigms are developed before the language features that make programming in them natural. We shouldn't be surprised, then, to find existing libraries, written in older programming languages, that use modern design techniques.

177

Because these techniques and design paradigms are not directly expressible in the syntax of the language in which they are coded, however, the library interface may be complicated or obscure. In these cases, we can create a C++ "envelope," or alternative interface to the library, that simplifies the existing interface or makes its design concepts explicit.

For example, consider the I/O functions provided in the C library `stdio`.

```
FILE *fopen( const char *, const char * );
int fclose( FILE * );
int fflush( FILE * );
int fprintf( FILE *, const char * ... );
int fscanf( FILE *, const char * ... );
```

One way to view these functions is as a collection of operations on file objects. Note that `fopen` fills the role of a constructor, `fclose` fills that of a destructor, and the other functions look just like member functions, even down to the (ordinarily) implicit `this` first argument.

We can define an alternative interface to make our abstraction explicit.

```
class File {
    FILE * const f;
  public:
    File( const char *path, const char *mode = "w" )
        : f( fopen( path, mode ) ) {}
    ~File() { fclose( f ); }
    int flush() { return fflush( f ); }
    int printf( const char * ... );
    int scanf( const char * ...);
};
```

The implementations of `File::printf` and `File::scanf` are complicated by the ellipsis final argument. We want the formal arguments in the definitions of the member `printf` and `scanf` functions to be used as the actual arguments to a call to the `stdio` functions `fprintf` and `fscanf`, respectively. As the ellipsis parameter tells us, however, we can't determine the number of arguments until runtime. There are several ways of dealing with this situation, most of which are environment dependent. Here in our minimal implementation of `File::printf` we use the "varargs" facility provided by definitions in the standard header `stdarg.h`. An object of type `va_list`, `ap` in our example, holds information on how to access the arguments. Note that `va_start` initializes `ap` using the last declared argument before the ellipsis, `fmt` in our example. In addition, `va_arg` returns successive arguments from the argument list interpreted according to the type provided in the second argument of va_arg. Finally, va_end provides a normal termination of the use of the variable-argument facility.

```
int
File::printf( const char *fmt ... ) {
    va_list ap;
    va_start( ap, fmt );

    register int c;
    while( c = *fmt++ ) {
        if( c == '%' ) {
            switch( c = *fmt++ ) {
            case 'c':    // character
                fprintf( f, "%c", va_arg( ap, int ) );
                break;
            case 'd':    // decimal integer
                fprintf( f, "%d", va_arg( ap, int ) );
                break;
            case 'g':    // floating
                fprintf( f, "%g", va_arg( ap, double ) );
                break;
            case 's':    // character string
                fprintf( f, "%s", va_arg( ap, char* ) );
                break;
            // etc...
            }
        }
        else
            fprintf( f, "%c", c );
    }

    va_end( ap );
}
```

Now we can create and use File objects for stdio. Note that we changed the name of the member output function from fprintf to printf, and the name of the member input function from fscanf to scanf, in order to match the names used for input and output to the predefined files stdout and stdin. Use of these routines can be thought of as I/O to default File objects.

```
void
tee( char *fn ) {
    File f = fn;
    char c;
    while( scanf( "%c", &c ) != EOF ) {
        f.printf( "%c", c );
        printf( "%c", c );
    }
}
```

8.2 Application-Oriented Languages

Special-purpose programming languages exist for simulation, string processing, numerical calculation, and so forth, with syntax and type system directed toward a specific problem domain. These languages exist because the custom language makes it easier to design, code, and maintain specialized application programs than would a more general-purpose language. Therefore the SNOBOL language allows its users to write compact string manipulation programs and APL allows its users to write compact matrix manipulation programs because these types are explicitly supported by each language. Users of these languages are free to design and code directly in the concepts with which their programs deal, rather than a lower-level representation.

Much of the functionality of an application-oriented language can be accomplished in C++ with class libraries. The complex arithmetic library defines a complex number data type, overloads existing arithmetic operators to supply the semantics of complex arithmetic, and defines conversions to and from existing arithmetic types to integrate the complex type into the predefined type system. In essence, the complex arithmetic library customizes the C++ *language* to a specialized application area. In a similar way the String library extends C++ to deal with character strings as if String were a built-in type.

It is difficult and expensive to implement a new programming language tailored to an application area, but class libraries are relatively easy to implement. It is therefore quite reasonable to design an application-oriented language library for an area in which relatively few programs are written or even for a single application. For example, if we are dealing with a bit-map graphics application, we would prefer to think of screen positions as distinct points rather than as Cartesian coordinate pairs.

```
class Point {
    short x, y;
  public:
    Point( int u, int v ) : x(u), y(v) {}
    Point operator -()
            { return Point(-x,-y); }
    Point operator +( Point p )
            { return Point(x+p.x,y+p.y); }
    Point operator -( Point p )
            { return Point(x-p.x,y-p.y); }
    Point operator *( int i )
            { return Point(x*i,y*i); }
    Point operator /( int i )
            { return Point(x/i,y/i); }
    Point operator %( int i )
            { return Point(x%i,y%i); }
    Point operator &( int i )
            { return Point(x&i,y&i); }
    Point operator +=( Point p )
            { return Point(x+=p.x,y+=p.y); }
    Point operator -=( Point p )
            { return Point(x-=p.x,y-=p.y); }
    int operator ==( Point p )
            { return x==p.x && y==p.y; }
    int operator !=( Point p )
            { return x!=p.x || y!=p.y; }
    int operator >=( Point p )
            { return x>=p.x && y>=p.y; }
    int operator <=( Point p )
            { return x<=p.x && y<=p.y; }
    int operator >( Point p )
            { return x>p.x && y>p.y; }
    int operator <( Point p )
            { return x<p.x && y<p.y; }
};
```

Now we can code as if C++ had a predefined Point type. For instance, rectangles can be defined in terms of points and operations on rectangles in terms of operations on points.

```
class Rectangle {
    Point origin, corner;
  public:
    Rectangle( Point p,  Point q)
        : origin(p), corner(q) {}
    Rectangle operator +( Point p )
        { return Rectangle(origin+p, corner+p); }
    Rectangle operator -( Point p )
        { return Rectangle(origin-p, corner-p); }
    Rectangle translate( Point p )
        { return Rectangle(p, corner+(p-origin)); }
    inline int operator <( Rectangle );
    inline int operator <=( Rectangle );
    Point center()
        { return (origin+corner)/2; }
    friend int operator <( Point, Rectangle );
    friend int operator <=( Point, Rectangle );
};

inline int
operator <( Point p, Rectangle r ) {
    return p>r.origin
        && p<(r.corner - Point (1,1));
}

inline int
operator <=( Point p, Rectangle r ) {
    return p>=r.origin
        && p<=(r.corner - Point (1,1));
}

inline int
operator >( Point p, Rectangle r ) {
    return !(p<=r);
}

inline int
Rectangle::operator <( Rectangle r ) {
    return origin<r && corner<r;
}

inline int
Rectangle::operator <=( Rectangle r ) {
    return origin<=r && corner<=r;
}
```

Rectangles can be used in turn to define windows and so on. At each point we design classes that allow us to design and code with the concepts we deal with, and not with a lower-level representation.

8.3 Extensible Libraries

All libraries are extensible in the sense that they can be used to produce other libraries. We call certain libraries extensible, however, if they are explicitly designed to be extended by users, through design of a framework for extensibility.

Consider the standard C++ library for stream I/O. The `streamio` library provides type secure input/output that is extensible to handle user-defined types. By contrast, the I/O facilities provided by the `stdio` library are not type secure.

```
#include <stdio.h>

extern int age;
extern String name;
printf( "%s's age is %d\n", age, name ); // oops!
```

This code is "correct" C++ but will produce garbage on execution, or possibly cause the program to bomb. The arguments `age` and `name` are in the wrong order for the format string, but the error is not detected because there is no type information available to tell the compiler that the format string expects first a `char *`, then an `int`. Even if we had gotten the arguments in the correct order, the print statement still would not work. The `printf` function expects a `char *` argument corresponding to the `%s` in the format string, but we've supplied a `String` argument. In the absence of type information, the C++ compiler does not know to supply the implicit conversion from `String` to `char *` (using `String::operator char *`). We could supply the necessary type information

```
inline int
age_print( char *f, char *n, int a ) {
    return printf( f, n, a );
}
//...
age_print( "%s's age is %d\n", name, age );
```

but this approach forces special-case handling of every printing situation.

A better approach is provided by the `streamio` library. Note that `streamio` overloads the operators `<<` and `>>` to provide type-secure output and input, respectively. The print statement above could be written as

```
cout << name << "'s age is " << age << "\n";
```

What follows is a simplified version of some of the features of the `streamio` library. First we define an output stream class, including left shift operators or "inserters" for inserting values onto the output stream.

```
typedef FILE *FP;
class ostream {
    FP f;
  public:
    ostream( FP fl ) : f( fl ) {}
    operator FP() { return f; }
    ostream &operator <<( char * );
    ostream &operator <<( int );
    ostream &operator <<( long );
    ostream &operator <<( double );
};

ostream cout = stdout;
```

For our simplified version, we use the `stdio` library to implement the semantics of our shift operators.

```
ostream &
ostream::operator <<( char *s ) {
    fprintf( f, "%s", s );
    return *this;
}
```

The definitions of the other instances of `ostream::operator <<` are similar. Note that each shift operator returns (a reference to) the `ostream` object for which it was invoked. This is what allows us to cascade several output operations into a single (noncomma) expression. Like most C++ operators, the shift operators are left associative, so the expression

```
cout << name << "'s age is " << age << "\n";
```

is parsed as

```
(((cout << name) << "'s age is ") << age) << "\n";
```

Because the `ostream` object `cout` is returned from each `operator <<`, this is equivalent to

```
cout << name;
cout << "'s age is ";
cout << age;
cout << "\n";
```

but is far easier to read.

An input stream can be created in a similar fashion, defining right shift operators or ''extractors'' for extracting values from the input stream.

```
class istream {
    FP f;
  public:
    istream( FP fl ) : f(fl) {}
    operator FP() { return f; }
    istream &operator >>( char * );
    istream &operator >>( int & );
    istream &operator >>( long & );
    istream &operator >>( double & );
    int gchar();     // get one char
};

istream &
istream::operator >>( long &l ) {
    fscanf( f, "%ld", &l );
    return *this;
}

istream cin = stdin;


cout << "Your age and name: ";
int age;
char nm[32];
cin >> age >> nm;
```

The classes ostream and istream form the basis of an extensible I/O library by defining I/O operations for C++'s predefined types, and by defining (by example) a syntax for input and output operations. This framework can be extended to user-defined types by defining additional overloaded shift operators. For example, we may want to do streamio of complex numbers.

```
class complex {
    double re, im;
  public:
    friend ostream &operator <<( ostream &, complex & );
    friend istream &operator >>( istream &, complex & );
    // ...
};
```

The friend declarations are necessary in this case to allow the shift operators access to the private representation of the complex number. The shift operators for complex I/O are defined in terms of the shift operators for the predefined types, just as complex itself is defined in terms of predefined types.

```
ostream &
operator <<( ostream &out, complex &c ) {
    out << "(" << c.re << "," << c.im << ")";
    return out;
}
```

```
istream &
operator >>( istream &in, complex &c ) {
    in >> ws;     // See Exercise 8-2.
    if( in.gchar() != '(' ) error();
    in >> c.re;
    in >> ws;
    if( in.gchar() != ',' ) error();
    in >> c.im;
    in >> ws;
    if( in.gchar() != ')' ) error();
    return in;
}
```

Note that the << operator outputs a complex number in a format that is acceptable to the >> operator for input.

How about output of a more complex user-defined type, like an abstract syntax tree? We would like to be able to write code like

```
extern Node *np;
cout << "The expression is: " << np;
```

to print a fully parenthesized infix representation of the tree whose root is referred to by np.

We approach the problem by first adding a virtual printing capability to the abstract syntax tree node hierarchy.

```
class Node {
    //...
    virtual void print( ostream & ) { error(); }
};

class Binop : public Node {
    //...
    virtual void print_op( ostream & ) { error(); }
    void print( ostream &out ) {
        out << "(";
        left->print( out );
        print_op( out );
        right->print( out );
        out << ")";
    }
};

class Plus : public Binop {
    //...
    void print_op( ostream &out ) { out << "+"; }
};

class Int : public Node {
    //...
    void print( ostream &out ) { out << value; }
};

// etc. ...
```

The operation of the virtual `print` routines is similar to that of the virtual `eval` routines and the virtual destructors already present in the abstract syntax tree node hierarchy. The routines recursively print the abstract syntax tree, calling the proper `print` routine based on the root node type of each subtree.

All that remains is to hook these member `print` routines up to the existing `streamio` library.

```
ostream &
operator <<( ostream &out, Node *np ) {
    np->print( out );
    return out;
}
```

In an earlier example, we requested user input and then waited for a response.

```
cout << "Your age and name: ";
```

Unfortunately, this may not work in the way we intend. If the output stream cout is buffered, the message to the user may wait (indefinitely) for the output buffer to fill before it is actually written. To get the correct behavior we should flush the cout buffer to ensure that the message is actually written.

```
cout << "Your age and name: ";
flush( cout );
```

Control signals of this kind interspersed with input and output operations adversely affect the readability of the code, however, and distract both the coder and reader from the program logic. We would prefer to write

```
cout << "Your age and name: " << flush;
```

We accomplish this with manipulators. A manipulator is a value in an expression that causes a side effect that is not strictly related to the major purpose of the expression. Typically, these values are function addresses.

```
ostream &flush( ostream & );
```

To allow such function addresses to be used in output expressions, we define an applicator (see Chapter 4) that applies its function (pointer) argument to the output stream and returns the output stream.

```
typedef ostream &(*MANIP)(ostream&);

inline ostream &
operator <<( ostream &out, MANIP f ) {
    return f( out );
}
```

This applicator allows any manipulator of type MANIP to be used in an output shift expression. Other applicators can be defined for manipulators with different types.

```
typedef int (*MANIP2)(FILE *);

inline ostream &
operator <<( ostream &out, MANIP2 f ) {
    f( out );
    return out;
}
```

```
extern int close( FILE * );

cout << "So long..." << flush << close;
```

It is frequently useful to allow parameterized manipulators. For instance, we may want to set various data transmission characteristics of an output stream to given argument values.

```
enum { odd, even, none };
enum { slow = 1200, lagom = 4800, fast = 9600 };

cout<<speed(fast)<<parity(none)<<"login: "<<flush;
```

In this case, the manipulator values are class objects that contain pairs of values: a function address and an integer argument value.

```
struct act_rec {
    void (*fp)(FILE *, int);
    int arg;
    act_rec( void (*f)(FILE *, int), int a )
        : fp(f), arg(a) {}
};
```

Note that speed and parity are functions that return act_recs.

```
inline act_rec
speed( int baudr ) {
    extern void set_speed( FILE *, int );
    return act_rec( set_speed, baudr );
}
```

Finally, we define an applicator that applies an act_rec to an ostream.

```
inline ostream &
operator <<( ostream &out, act_rec m ) {
    m.fp( out, m.arg );
    return out;
}
```

8.4 Customizable Libraries

Often a library provides a service that comes close to what is needed for an application without being exactly suitable. In these cases it is helpful if the library is designed to be customizable.

Consider the abstract syntax tree node hierarchy of Chapter 5. This library provides a general abstraction of a binary operator, so it is easy to extend the library through inheritance to handle additional binary operators.

```
class And : public Binop {
  public:
    And( Node *l, Node *r ) : Binop(l,r) {}
    int eval() { return left->eval() & right->eval(); }
};
```

All we have to do to add a new binary operator is to augment the general abstraction with the specifics of the particular operator we are adding.

The library does not contain an abstraction of a unary operator, however, but only a specific unary minus. Adding a new unary operator forces a user of the library to do a lot more work, including the definition of general properties of unary operators (like destructor semantics) as well as properties of the specific unary operator being added.

```
class Uplus : public Node {
    Node *operand;
  public:
    Uplus( Node *o ) { operand = o; }
    ~Uplus() { delete operand; }
    int eval() { return operand->eval(); }
};
```

Most of this class definition would not have been necessary if a general unary operator abstraction were present in the library. Not only does the absence of such an abstraction force users of the library to write more code than they would otherwise, but it requires that they know more about the details of the library implementation. For libraries with complex implementations it is unlikely that naive users will get all the details correct. In general, one cannot foresee how a given library may be used or customized, and all levels of abstraction should be made explicit.

Another use of inheritance for customization is to create alternate versions of existing types. For instance, we may want a version of ostream that can be initialized with a pathname of a file and that prohibits copying in order to avoid accidental aliasing of files.

```
class ostr : public ostream {
  public:
    ostr( char *path ) : ostream( fopen(path,"w") ) {}
    ~ostr() { fclose( FP( *this ) ); }
  private:
    ostr( ostr & );
    void operator =( ostr & );
};
```

Class `ostr` inherits the `<<` and `FP` operators from its `ostream` base class and, because it *is* an `ostream` (i.e., `ostream` is a public base class of `ostr`), can be used anywhere an `ostream` can. We have made `X(X&)` and `operator` = private operations to prevent copying of `ostr`s.

We can also use inheritance to merge and customize multiple classes.

```
class iostream : public istream, public ostream {
  public:
    iostream( FILE *fp ) : istream(fp), ostream(fp) {}
};
```

An `iostream` can be used for both insertion and extraction, because it inherits the properties of both `istream` and `ostream`. To make `iostream`s useful for random-access I/O, we can create a `seek` manipulator in a manner similar to that for the `speed` and `parity` manipulators described earlier.

```
extern iostream cfile;
extern char first, fifth, replacement;

cfile >> first >> seek(5) >> fifth;
cfile << replacement;
```

8.5 Exercises

Exercise 8-1. †Write a manipulator and applicator for class `complex` to do rounding for additions:

```
extern complex a, b, c, d, e;
d = a + b + round + c + round;
```

Write an analogous manipulator that does the same operation for (predefined) integer expressions. □

Exercise 8-2. Write an `istream` manipulator and applicator that consumes (discards) white space: `cin >> ws;` □

Exercise 8-3. We've seen manipulators that are function addresses and pairs of values. Devise examples of other types of values that could be used as manipulators, and write applicators that apply them in `istream`, `ostream`, `String`, and `complex` expressions. □

Exercise 8-4. †Write an inserter for the `sorted_collection` type of Chapter 4. Do not change the implementation or interface of the `sorted_collection`. □

Exercise 8-5. Write an extractor for abstract syntax trees, corresponding to the inserter described in this chapter. You cannot assume the input is fully parenthesized, however. (Hint: What is the difference between a parser for the calculator language of Chapter 5 and this extractor?) □

Exercise 8-6. Develop a library to make C++ into an application-oriented language for vector and matrix arithmetic. □

Exercise 8-7. Design a library for a relational database algebra. Implement two interfaces to the database operators, one that uses infix operators, and another that uses function call syntax. (Hint: How will you represent properties for searches as abstract syntax trees? What's the difference between database access software and a programming language interpreter?) Design control structures (such as iterators) to extend your relational algebra to a relational calculus. □

Exercise 8-8. Given the definitions of `istream` and `ostream` in this chapter, explain the semantics of the following two expressions:

```
cout << 12;
cin >> 12;
```

Given the definition of `iostream` in this chapter, explain why the expression `cfile >> first << replacement` won't compile. Redesign the implementation of `iostream` so that mixed I/O expressions like this are legal. □

Exercise 8-9. Are `<<` and `>>` good choices for the `streamio` insertion and extraction operators? Why or why not? What other operator(s) would be good choices? Why is `->` a bad choice? Why is `=` a terrible choice? □

Exercise 8-10. Show how the use of inheritance to customize class types can be used to fix library bugs without altering the library source. Use this technique to circumvent the environment-dependent order of evaluation of the operands of binary abstract syntax tree nodes in the `eval` function, as pointed out in the solution to Exercise 5-3. ☐

Exercise 8-11. †Often a library requires initialization before use. Design a scheme that will ensure that a library is initialized (once) in any application in which it is included. ☐

Exercise 8-12. Some customizable libraries are designed to be "application frameworks," that is, blank applications that are customized to produced a family of real applications.

Refer to Exercise 6-5. Design an application framework for applications that are modeled as a sequence of state transitions. Implement an airline reservation system, a lexical analyzer for C++, and the finite state automaton abstract data type of Exercise 4-8 by using inheritance to customize your framework. ☐

APPENDIX: **Solved Exercises**

Exercise 1-3.

```
a        // int
b        // int *
*b       // int
c        // int *
*c       // int
d[2]     // int *
*d       // int *
**d      // int
c[-2]    // int
c-2      // int *
*(c-2)   // int
&c       // int **
```

□

Exercise 1-4.

```
c = cc;          // legal
cc = c;          // illegal
pcc = &c;        // legal
pcc = &cc;       // legal
pc = &c;         // legal
pc = &cc;        // illegal
pc = pcc;        // illegal
pc = cpc;        // legal
pc = cpcc;       // illegal
cpc = pc;        // illegal
*cpc = *pc;      // legal
pc = *pcpc;      // legal
**pcpc = *pc;    // legal
*pc = **pcpc;    // legal
```

□

Exercise 2-4.

```
char *
get_token( char *&s, char *ws = " \t\n" ) {
    char *p;
    do
        for( p = ws; *p && *s != *p; p++ );
    while( *p ? *s++ : 0 );
    char *ret = s;
    do
        for( p = ws; *p && *s != *p; p++ );
    while( *p ? 0 : *s ? s++ : 0 );
    return ret;
}


int strlen( char *s ) {
    char *t = get_token( s, "" );
    return s-t;
}
```

☐

Exercise 3-1. A union is used to get at the bit representation of the double argument.

```
void
bitprint( double val ) {
    static int nbitsinchar = 0;
    if( !nbitsinchar ) {
        // calculate number of bits in a char
        for( unsigned c = 1; c; c <<= 1 )
            nbitsinchar++;
    }
    union {
        double d;
        unsigned char a[ sizeof(double) ];
    };
    d = val;
    for( int i = 0; i < sizeof(double); i++ ) {
        unsigned c = a[i];
        for( int j = nbitsinchar; j; j-- )
            if( c & ( 1 << j ) )
                printf("1");
            else
                printf("0");
    }
}
```

□

Exercise 3-2. A hash table class, Htab, could be implemented as follows using a list to store records that hash to the same point:

```
class Rec {
    // details...
  public:
    char *key;
};

class Clist {    // hash table collision list
    Rec *r;
    Clist *next;
    friend Htab;
};
```

```
class Htab {      // hash table type
    Clist **tab;      // ptr to table
    int hash(char *);
    int size;    // size of table
  public:
    Rec *insert(Rec *);
    Rec *lookup(char *);
    Rec *remove(char *);
    Htab(int);
    ~Htab();
};

Htab::Htab( int sz )
    : size(sz), tab( new Clist *[size] ) {}

Htab::~Htab() {
    for( int i = 0; i < size; i++ ) {
        Clist *p = tab[i], *q;
        while( p ) {
            q = p;
            p = p->next;
            delete q;
        }
    }
    delete [size] tab;
}

Rec *
Htab::lookup( char *s ) {
    // Return ptr to record, 0 on failure.
    for( Clist *p = tab[hash(s)]; p; p = p->next )
        if( strcmp( s, p->r->key ) == 0 )
            return p->r;
    return 0;
}
```

```
Rec *
Htab::insert( Rec *r ) {
    // Return ptr to inserted record, 0 on failure.
    if( lookup( r->key ) )
        return 0;
    int i = hash( r->key );
    Clist *p = new Clist;
    p->r = r;
    p->next = tab[i];
    tab[i] = p;
    return r;
}


Rec *
Htab::remove( char *s ) {
    // Return ptr to removed record, 0 on failure.
    int i = hash( s );
    Clist *p = tab[i], *q = 0;
    while( p && strcmp( p->r->key, s ) ) {
        q = p;
        p = p->next;
    }
    if( p ) {
        if( q )
            q->next = p->next;
        else
            tab[i] = p->next;
        Rec *r = p->r;
        delete p;
        return r;
    }
    else
        return 0;
}
```

Htab::hash could be implemented like the hash function in Chapter 1, Section 3. □

Exercise 3-4. We define a trace class type that is initialized with the name of the function or block in which it is declared.

```
class trace {
    char * const msg;
  public:
    trace( char *m ) : msg( m ) {
        fprintf( stderr, "entering %s\n", msg );
    }
    ~trace() {
        fprintf( stderr, "leaving %s\n", msg );
    }
};
```

The declaration of a `trace` object causes the constructor to print an "entering . . ." message when the object comes into scope. When the object goes out of scope, the destructor prints a "leaving . . ." message. Explain how the trace objects work on the following code:

```
void
buggy_func( int arg ) {
    trace a = "buggy_func";
    if( arg ) {
        trace b = "then part";
        //...
        return;
    }
    else {
        trace c = "else part";
        //...
    }
}
```

☐

Exercise 4-14. An associative array maps index values to elements of the array. According to this definition, a standard C++ array is associative: it maps integers to array elements. Another example of an associative array is a compiler symbol table, because it maps identifiers to their attributes. Our associative array is going to map `String`s to `String`s, so both the index and element type are `String`.

```
typedef String I;
typedef String E;
```

To implement the mapping from `String` to `String` we create an associative array class and overload the `[]` operator to allow us to index our associative array as if it were a regular array.

```
class Pair {
    I index;
    E el;
    Pair *next;
    friend Aary;
};
class Aary {
    Pair *elems;
  public:
    Aary() { elems = 0; }
    E &operator[]( I );
};
```

For this implementation, our array is just a list of index, element pairs. Note that `operator[]` performs a linear search of the list each time the associative array is indexed. This is appropriate for arrays with few indices, but for large arrays a more efficient search method is called for (hash table, balanced tree, and so on)

```
E &
Aary ::operator[]( I i ) {
    for( Pair *p = elems; p; p = p->next )
        if( p->index == i )
            return p->el;
    p = new Pair;
    p->index = i;
    p->next = elems;
    elems = p;
    return p->el;
}
```

Note that `operator[]` creates an element on access if it does not exist already. Now we can declare and use our dictionary type.

```
Aary dict;
dict["cat"]   = "meow";
dict["dog"]   = "moo";
dict["cow"]   = "woof";
dict["sheep"] = "baa";
dict["dog"]   = dict["cow"];
dict["cow"]   = "moo";
```

Our implementation imposes very few constraints on the index and element types. The index type must have the operators `==` and `=` defined, and the element type must have the operator `=` defined. In addition, both types must be able to be declared without an initializer, or have a default initializer.

We take advantage of these observations and make our type generic, using the macros defined in the library generic.h.

```
#include <generic.h>
#define Pair(I,E)  name3(I,E,Pair)
#define Aary(I,E)  name3(I,E,Aary)
#define Aarydeclare2(I,E) \
class Pair(I,E) { \
    I index; \
    E el; \
    Pair(I,E) *next; \
    friend Aary(I,E); \
}; \
class Aary(I,E) { \
    Pair(I,E) *elems; \
  public: \
    Aary(I,E)() { elems = 0; } \
    E &operator[]( I ); \
}; \
static E & \
Aary(I,E)::operator[]( I i ) { \
    for( Pair(I,E) *p = elems; p; p = p->next ) \
        if( p->index == i ) \
            return p->el; \
    p = new Pair(I,E); \
    p->index = i; \
    p->next = elems; \
    elems = p; \
    return p->el; \
}
```

Now we can instantiate versions of our generic type and declare objects of the instantiated type.

We can start by instantiating our dictionary type.

```
declare2(Aary,String,String);
```

We can use the preprocessor macro Aary declared above to generate the type name of our dictionary each time we use it

```
Aary(String,String) dict;
```

or we can use a typedef name:

```
typedef Aary(String,String) Dictionary;
Dictionary dict;
```

We can create an associative array type that maps Strings to Dictionarys by instantiating another version of our generic associative array type.

```
declare2(Aary,String,Dictionary);
typedef Aary(String,Dictionary) Library;
Library lib;
lib["barnyard"] = dict;
```

Other instantiations might include a compiler symbol table

```
declare2(Aary,String,Nameinfo);
typedef Aary(String,Nameinfo) Symtab;
```

or a very large, sparse array with integer indicies.

```
declare2(Aary,long,Type);
typedef Aary(long,Type) Large_ary;
Large_ary a;
Type x, y, z;
a[0] = x;
a[1000000000] = y;
a[2000000000] = z;
```

□

Exercise 4-16. We use the old trick of using exclusive OR to encode the bits for both the previous and next link pointers into a single pointer. We can recover the the address of the previous element from the encoding if we have the address of the next element and conversely.

```
encoded = previous ^ next;
next == encoded ^ previous;
previous == encoded ^ next;
```

To traverse the list in either direction, all we need are unencoded addresses for the head and tail of the list.

```
typedef int ETYPE;
typedef int BITS;

class list_el {
    list_el *ptr;
    ETYPE el;
    friend list;
    friend iter;
    friend void paste( list_el *&, list_el *&, ETYPE );
};
```

```
class list {
    list_el *hd, *tl;
  public:
    list() { hd = tl = 0; }
    friend list &operator +( list &, ETYPE );
    friend list &operator =( ETYPE, list & );
    list_el *head() { return hd; }
    list_el *tail() { return tl; }
    friend iter;
};
```

We overload the = operator to add an element at the head of the list, and the + operator to add an element to the end of the list.

```
list &
operator +( list &lst, ETYPE e ) {
    paste( lst.tl, lst.hd, e );
    return lst;
}

list &
operator =( ETYPE e, list &lst ) {
    paste( lst.hd, lst.tl, e );
    return lst;
}


void
paste( list_el *&front, list_el *&back, ETYPE e ) {
    list_el *tmp = new list_el;
    tmp->el = e;
    if( !front )
        back = front = tmp;
    else if( back == front ) {
        back->ptr = front = tmp;
        tmp->ptr = back;
    }
    else {
        tmp->ptr = front;
        front->ptr =
            (list_el *)(BITS(front->ptr) ^ BITS(tmp));
        front = tmp;
    }
}
```

An iterator object is initialized with the end of the list at which the traversal is to start.

```
class iter {
    list_el *prev, *curr;
  public:
    iter( list_el *start ) { prev = 0; curr = start; }
    ETYPE *operator () ();
};


ETYPE *
iter::operator () () {
    if( !curr )
        return 0;
    list_el *tmp = curr;
    curr = (list_el *)(BITS(curr->ptr) ^ BITS(prev));
    prev = tmp;
    return &tmp->el;
}
```

Now we can create lists and traverse them in either direction.

```
typedef int ETYPE;
#include "list.h"

main() {
    int *ip;
    list ints;
    1 = 2 = 3 = ints + 4 + 5 + 6;

    iter forw = ints.head();
    while( ip = forw() )
        printf( "%d ", *ip );

    iter backw = ints.tail();
    while( ip = backw() )
        printf( "%d ", *ip );
}
```

Although the integers in the list are in ascending order, they are added to the list in the order 4, 5, 6, 3, 2, 1. Why? What do you think about our use of the = operator for adding elements to the head of the list? Is this a good idea?

One important aspect of this solution to the problem is that the encoded representation of the forward and backward links is hidden from users of the list. When we come to our senses later and decide to use separate forward and backward link pointers, we can make the change without affecting the code that uses the list. □

Exercise 5-3. First we define an identifier node type and a symbol table to map identifiers to values. Because there are no declarations in our calculator language, we create a symbol table entry for a name the first time its identifier is used.

```
class Nament {
    char *name;
    int value;
    Nament *next;
    Nament( char *nm, nament *n ) {
        name = strcpy( new char[ strlen(nm)+1 ], nm );
        value
        value = 0;
        next = n;
    }
    friend Id;
};

class Id : public Node {
    static Nament *symtab;
    Nament *entry;
    Nament *look(char *);
  public:
    Id( char *nm ) { entry = look( nm ); }
    int set( int i ) { return entry->value = i; }
    int eval() { return entry->value; }
};
```

```
Nament *
Id::look( char *nm ) {
    for( Nament *p = symtab; p; p = p->next )
        if( strcmp( p->name, nm ) == 0 )
            return p;
    return symtab = new Nament( nm, symtab );
}
```

Next, we define an assignment node type.

```
class Assign : public Binop {
  public:
    Assign( Id *t, Node *e ) : Binop( t, e ) {}
    int eval()
        { return ((Id *)left)->set( right->eval() ); }
};
```

Note that we have to cast the left pointer in order to invoke Id::set in Assign::eval. Why? We could avoid the cast by declaring set to be a virtual member function in `Node`. Why is this a bad idea?

Ordinarily, we should not have to change the implementations of the other abstract syntax tree node types to accommodate the addition of the assignment operator. We made an *implicit* assumption in the implementation of the other binary operators, however, that evaluation order does not matter. Let us look at the implementation of `Plus::eval`.

```
int
Plus::eval() {
    return left->eval() + right->eval();
}
```

Recall that C++ does not completely define the evaluation order of expressions. Therefore we cannot say whether the left or the right subtree of the addition will be evaluated first. This is generally all right if the expression being evaluated has no side effects, but assignment statements do have side effects. Consider the effect of evaluating the right subtree of an addition before the left subtree in the following expression: `(id = 12) + id`. A more portable implementation of `Plus::eval` would be

```
int
Plus::eval() {
    int l = left->eval();
    return l + right->eval();
}
```

An implementation of an interactive calculator that uses our abstract syntax tree hierarchy is given below.

```
#include <stdio.h>
#include <string.h>
#include <ctype.h>
#include "Nodes.h"

static int token;    // current token
static char lexeme[81]; // attribute for ID and INT
enum { ID = 257, INT, EOLN, BAD };

Node *E(), *T(), *F();
```

```
/*
    Scanner:  return the next token in the input stream.
        attributes for integer constants and identifiers
        dumped in global variable "lexeme".
*/
int
scan() {
    int c;
    while( 1 )
        switch( c = getchar() ) {
        case '+': case '-':
        case '*': case '/':
        case '(': case ')':
        case '=':
            return c;
        case ' ': case '\t':
            continue;
        case '\n':
            return EOLN;
        default:
            if( isdigit( c ) ) {
                char *s = lexeme;
                do
                    *s++ = c;
                while( isdigit( c = getchar() ) );
                *s = '\0';
                ungetc( c, stdin );
                return INT;
            }
            if( isalpha( c ) ) {
                char *s = lexeme;
                do
                    *s++ = c;
                while( isalnum(c = getchar()) );
                *s = '\0';
                ungetc( c, stdin );
                return ID;
            }
            return BAD;
        }
}
```

```
/*
    On error, just give up.
*/
void
error() {
    printf( "ERROR!!!\n" );
    exit( 255 );
}
/*
    Predictive parser for a simple expression grammar:

        E --> T {(+|-)T}
        T --> F {(*|/)F}
        F --> ID | INT | ( E ) | ID = E | -F
*/

Node *
E() {
    Node *root = T();
    while( 1 )
        switch( token ) {
        case '+':
            token = scan();
            root = new Plus( root, T() );
            break;
        case '-':
            token = scan();
            root = new Minus( root, T() );
            break;
        default:
            return root;
        }
}
```

```
Node *
F() {
    Node *root;
    switch( token ) {
    case ID:
        root = new Id( lexeme );
        token = scan();
        if( token == '=' ) {
            token = scan();
            root = new Assign( (Id *)root, E() );
        }
        return root;
    case INT:
        root = new Int( atoi( lexeme ) );
        token = scan();
        return root;
    case '(':
        token = scan();
        root = E();
        if( token != ')' )
            error();
        token = scan();
        return root;
    case '-':
        token = scan();
        return new Uminus( F() );
    default:
        error();
    }
}
```

```
Node *
T() {
    Node *root = F();
    while( 1 )
        switch( token ) {
        case '*':
            token = scan();
            root = new Times( root, F() );
            break;
        case '/':
            token = scan();
            root = new Div( root, F() );
            break;
        default:
            return root;
        }
}


/*
    Driver:  initialize, loop while no error.
*/
main() {
    Node *root;
    while( 1 ) {
        token = scan();
        if( (root = E()) && token == EOLN ) {
            printf( "%d\n", root->eval() );
            delete root;
        }
        else
            error();
    }
}
```

☐

Exercise 5-7. d) First we modify the constructor and destructor for Node, the root class of our abstract syntax tree hierarchy, to keep track of the number of nodes allocated. It is sufficient to modify only the constructor and destructor for Node, because these are invoked any time a constructor or destructor for any class derived from Node is invoked.

```
class Node {
  protected:
    Node() { num_nodes++; }
  public:
    ~Node() { num_nodes--; }
    virtual int eval();
    static long num_nodes;
};
```

Now we can derive a new monitor type that monitors the number of nodes.

```
class Nalloc : public Monitor {
    long max_nodes;
  public:
    double get_value() {
        return Node::num_nodes > max_nodes
                ? max_nodes
                : Node::num_nodes;
    }
    Nalloc( long max = 1000 ) :
        Monitor( "Nodes", 0, max, 0.5 ),
        max_nodes( max ) {}
};
```

□

Exercise 6-4. Simulation with central control of multiple airports:

```
#include "task.h"

class Airport;

class Plane : object {
    static int fltcount;
    long start;
    int fltno;
    Airport *origin;
    Airport *destination;
  public:
    Plane( Airport *o, Airport *d ) {
        fltno = ++fltcount;
        origin = o;
        destination = d;
    }
    long howlong() { return clock - start; }
    void set() { start = clock; }
    int flt() { return fltno; }
    Airport *to() { return destination; }
    Airport *from() { return origin; }
    void reschedule();
};

class PlaneQ {
    qhead *head;
    qtail *tail;
  public:
    PlaneQ() {  head = new qhead( ZMODE, 50 );
                tail = head->tail();}
    void put( Plane *p ) { p->set();
                tail->put( (object*)p );}
    Plane *get() { return (Plane *)head->get(); }
    int isroom() { return tail->rdspace(); }
    int notempty() { return head->rdcount(); }
};
```

```
class AirControl : public task   {
    PlaneQ  *landing, *inair, *incoming, *outgoing;
    PlaneQ  *incircling, *outcircling;
    int ok_take_off;
  public:
    AirControl( PlaneQ*, PlaneQ*, PlaneQ*, PlaneQ* );
    ~AirControl();
    int tok() { return ok_take_off; }
};

class GroundControl : public task {
    PlaneQ *takingoff, *onground;
  public:
    GroundControl( PlaneQ*, PlaneQ* );
};

class Airport : public task {
    PlaneQ  *takingoff, *landing, *inair,
        *onground, *incoming, *outgoing;
    AirControl *acontrol;
    GroundControl *gcontrol;
    const int index;
    char * const nm;
  public:
    Airport( PlaneQ *, PlaneQ*, int, char* );
    ~Airport();
    char *name() { return nm; }
    friend CentralControl;
};

class CentralControl : public task {
    static nairports;
    static Airport **airports;
    static urand *acity;
  public:
    CentralControl();
    ~CentralControl();
    friend Airport *pickacity() {
        return CentralControl::
            airports[CentralControl::acity->draw()];}
};
```

```
Airport::Airport( PlaneQ *in, PlaneQ *out,
                int i, char *id ) :
    incoming(in), outgoing(out), index(i), nm(id) {

    takingoff = new PlaneQ;
    inair = new PlaneQ;
    landing = new PlaneQ;
    onground = new PlaneQ;
    acontrol = new AirControl( landing, inair,
                    incoming, outgoing );
    gcontrol = new GroundControl( takingoff,onground);
    Plane *tp=0, *lp=0; // waiting planes
    int maxwait = 30;
    for(;;){
        delay( 10 );
        if( !lp ) lp = landing->get();
        if( !tp && acontrol->tok() ) tp = takingoff->get();
        if( lp ){
            if( onground->isroom() ) {
                printf("flight %d from %s landing at %s\n",
                    lp->flt(), lp->from()->name(), name());
                onground->put( lp );
                lp = 0;
            }
            else if( lp->howlong() > maxwait ) {
                printf("flight %d crash landing at %s!\n",
                    lp->flt(), name());
                delete lp;
                lp = 0;
            } else
                printf("flight %d landing at %s delayed\n",
                    lp->flt(), name());
        }
        if( tp ) {
            if( inair->isroom() ) {
                printf("flight %d from %s to %s taking off\n",
                    tp->flt(), name(), tp->to()->name());
                inair->put( tp );
                tp = 0;
            } else
                printf("flight %d take off from %s delayed\n",
                    lp ->flt(), name() );
            }
    } // end for(;;)
}
```

```
AirControl::AirControl( PlaneQ *land, PlaneQ *ina,
               PlaneQ *income, PlaneQ *outgo) :
    landing(land), inair(ina),
               incoming(income), outgoing(outgo) {
    incircling = new PlaneQ;
    outcircling = new PlaneQ;
    Plane *ip = 0, *op = 0;
    ok_take_off = 1;
    for(;;){
        delay( 10 );
        while(inair->notempty() && outcircling->isroom())
            outcircling->put( inair->get() );
        while(incoming->notempty() && incircling->isroom())
            incircling->put( incoming->get() );
        if (!ip ) ip = incircling->get();
        if( !op ) op = outcircling->get();
        if( ip ) {
            if( landing->isroom() ) {
                printf("flight %d arriving at %s\n",
                    ip->flt(), ip->to()->name() );
                landing->put( ip );
                ip = 0;
            }
            else {
                printf("flight %d delayed circling %s\n",
                    ip->flt(), ip->to()->name() );
            }
        }
        if( op ) {
            if( outgoing->isroom() ) {
                printf("flight %d leaving %s airspace\n",
                    op->flt(), op->from()->name() );
                outgoing->put( op );
                ok_take_off = 1;
                op = 0;
            }
            else {
                printf("flight %d delayed circling %s\n",
                    op->flt(), op->from()->name() );
                ok_take_off = 0;
            }
        }
    } // end for(;;)
}
```

```
CentralControl::CentralControl() {

    const int n = 9;
    nairports = n;
    acity = new urand ( 0, n-1 );
    static char *nms[ n ] = {
        "New York", "Newark", "Chicago",
        "Denver", "Columbus", "Austin",
        "Dallas", "Los Angeles", "Portland",
    };
    airports = new Airport*[n];
    for( int i = 0; i < n; i++ ) {
        airports[ i ] =
            new Airport(new PlaneQ,new PlaneQ,i,nms[i]);
    }

    // give each airport some planes
    urand nplanes( 20, 40 );
    for( i = 0; i < n; i++ ) {
        Airport *port = airports[ i ];
        for( int m = nplanes.draw(); m;   m-- )
            port->onground->put( new Plane( 0, port ) );
    }

    // direct air traffic between airports
    // schedule new flights from empty airports
    for(;;) {
        delay( 10 );
        for( i = 0; i < n; i++ ) {
            Airport *port = airports[ i ];
            Plane *p = port->outgoing->get();
            if( p )
                if( p->to()->incoming->isroom() )
                    p->to()->incoming->put( p );
                else {
                    printf("flight %d crashed",
                        p->flt() );
                    delete p;
                }
            if( !port->onground->notempty() ) {
                port->onground->put(new Plane(0,port));
            }
        }
    } // end for(;;)
}
```

```
AirControl::~AirControl() {
    while( incircling->notempty()
            && incoming->notempty() )
        thistask->delay( 10 );
    Plane *p;
    while( p = outcircling->get() )
        incircling->put( p );
    while( incircling->notempty() )
        thistask->delay( 10 );
    cancel( 0 );
}


GroundControl::GroundControl( PlaneQ *takingoff,
                    PlaneQ *onground ) {
    urand n( 10, 30 );
    Plane *p = 0;
    for(;;){
        delay( n.draw() );
        if( !p ) p = onground->get();
        if( p ) {
            if( takingoff->isroom() ) {
                p->reschedule(); // set new destination
                printf("flight %d leaving %s gate\n",
                        p->flt(), p->from()->name() );
                takingoff->put( p );
                p = 0;
            } else
                printf("flight %d delayed at %s gate\n",
                        p->flt(), p->from()->name() );
        }
    } // end for(;;)
}

void
Plane::reschedule() {
    origin = destination;
    destination = pickacity();
    start = clock;
}
```

```
Airport::~Airport() {
    gcontrol->cancel(0);
    delete acontrol;
    while( landing->notempty() )
        thistask->delay( 10 );
    printf("%s Airport Closed\n", name() );
    cancel(0);
}

CentralControl::~CentralControl() {
    for( int i = 0; i < nairports ; i++ ) {
        delete airports[ i ];
    }
    printf("CentralControl Closed\n");
    cancel( 0 );
}


main() {
    CentralControl *ccp = new CentralControl;
    thistask->delay( 5000 );
    delete ccp;
    thistask->resultis(0);
}
```

□

Exercise 7-2. Here is one implementation.

```
typedef void (*CTOR)( void * );
typedef void (*DTOR)( void *, int );

void *
_vec_new( void *vthis, int n, int sz, void *f ) {
    if( vthis == 0 )
        vthis = new char[n*sz];
    register char *p = (char *) vthis;
    if( f )
        for( register int i = 0; i < n; i++ )
            ( *CTOR(f) )( p+i*sz );
    return p;
}
```

```
void
_vec_delete( void *vthis, int n, int sz, void *f, int del )
    if( vthis == 0 )
        return;
    if( f ) {
        register char* p = (char *) vthis;
        for( register int i = 0; i < n; i++)
            ( *DTOR(f) )( p+i*sz, 0 );
    }
    if( del )
        delete vthis;
}
```

□

Exercise 7-7. We use the macros in `generic.h` to create a generic pointer type that is instantiated with the type of object to which it refers:

```
#define Hptr(ETYPE) name2(ETYPE,Hptr)

#define Hptrdeclare(ETYPE) \
class Hptr(ETYPE) { \
    ETYPE *p; \
  public: \
    Hptr(ETYPE)( ETYPE *v = 0 ) { p = v; } \
    operator ETYPE *() { return p; } \
    ETYPE &operator *() { \
        check(p); \
        return *p; \
    } \
    ETYPE &operator[]( long i ) { \
        check(p+i); \
        return p[i]; \
    } \
    Hptr(ETYPE) &operator ++() { \
        p++; \
        return *this; \
    } \
    // etc. ... \
};
```

Our generic pointer is implemented as a regular pointer to the type with which the generic pointer is instantiated. We supply all the usual arithmetic operations on pointers (although we show only ++ above) by performing the operation on regular pointer in the representation. The operations * and [] check the pointer address, however, before dereferencing to ensure that it refers to free store.

The implementation of the routine that performs this check is highly dependent on the environment in which our pointer type is used. Under Unix, the system call `sbrk` can be used to find the current bounds of free store.

```
static char *ilimit;
class Hptr_init {
    // See Exercise 8-11.
  public:
    Hptr_init() { ilimit = sbrk(0); }
};
static Hptr_init init;

void
check( void *p ) {
    if( p < ilimit || p >= sbrk(0) )
        error();
}
```

Alternatively, greater efficiency and a measure of environment independence is possible if operators `new` and `delete` have been redefined. In this case, `new` and `delete` can maintain a list of starting and ending addresses of free store blocks, obviating the need for `check` to perform a system call each time a smart pointer is dereferenced.

Our pointer type as defined above can be instantiated with any type, so we can have safe heap pointers to predefined types like `char`s and `double`s as well as class types.

```
Hptrdeclare(char);
typedef Hptr(char) cHptr;

Hptrdeclare(double);
typedef Hptr(double) dHptr;

struct Pair {
    int i, j;
};
Hptrdeclare(Pair);
typedef Hptr(Pair) PHptr;
PHptr PP;
```

Our generic pointer does not provide an `operator ->` because `->` cannot be used with pointers to nonclass types. Therefore, to access a member of a `Pair` with a `PHptr`, we must use the syntax `(*PP).i` rather than `PP->i`. We could augment our generic pointer type to allow the `->` operator, but then it could no longer be instantiated with nonclass types.

In providing the solution to this exercise, we have taken some liberties in interpreting the statement of the problem. We were to design a generic pointer that is guaranteed to point only to free store, but we have implemented a pointer that can only *reference* free store. The pointer can contain any address at all; the address contained in the pointer is only checked just before it is dereferenced with a `*` or `[]`.

This could be a problem, because we have provided a conversion operator that allows conversion to the corresponding regular pointer type.

```
char *strcpy(char *, char *);
cHptr s;
char *t;
strcpy( s, t );
```

The conversion could allow the address contained in the pointer to be used even if it did not refer to free store.

We could approach this problem by getting rid of the conversion operator, but this would reduce the utility of our type, because we could no longer use objects of the type as actual arguments and operands to existing functions and operators that are declared to work with the corresponding regular pointer types. Our generic pointer type would not be integrated into the predefined type system.

Alternatively, we could assure that the value of the pointer always referred to free store by checking the value after each initialization, assignment, and arithmetic operation, instead of on dereferencing. This would (occasionally) prevent our pointer type from being used in any algorithm that attempts to reference past the end of a data structure, however, if the data structure is at the end of free store.

```
int
strlen2( cHptr s ) {
    // return length of string, including '\0'
    cHptr t = s;
    while( *t++ );
    return t-s;
}
```

Because t eventually contains an address past the end of the character string to which s refers, it could conceivably be a nonfree store address.

Is it possible to say which of these approaches is correct, or are there situations in which each of these approaches is preferred to the others? □

Exercise 8-1. We assume we have available a function that rounds a complex value:

```
complex round( complex );
```

All we have to do is supply the appropriate applicator.

```
inline complex
operator +( complex val, complex (*manip)(complex) ) {
    return manip( val );
}
```

Providing the same functionality for integer expressions requires a different approach. Recall that a user-defined operator must have at least one class type argument. Because `ints` do not have class type, we have to make the other argument to `operator +` have class type. Here's one way:

```
int int_round( int );

class ROUND {};
ROUND iround;

inline int
operator +( int ival, ROUND dummy ) {
    return int_round( ival );
}
```

☐

Exercise 8-4. Because `sorted_collection` already has a way of applying a function to each element of the collection in the correct order, we use that. Unfortunately, the `apply` function can only take an argument of type `void (*) (ETYPE)`, so we must devise a way to pass the `ostream` to the apply function.

```
static ostream *oarg;

void
print( ETYPE e ) {
    *oarg << e;
    *oarg << " ";
}

ostream &
operator <<( ostream &out, sorted_collection &sc ) {
    out << "{ ";
    oarg = &out;    // kludge...
    apply( print );
    out << "}";
    return out;
}
```

What are the potential problems with this solution? How would you solve it if you could change the interface to `sorted_collection`? □

Exercise 8-11. Here's one solution: We create an initialization type whose constructor initializes the library. We declare a static object of the initialization type in the library source (*not* the header file!)

```
class lib_init {
  public:
    lib_init() {
        // lib init code...
    }
    ~lib_init() {
        // lib cleanup code...
    }
};

static lib_init init;
```

The implicit constructor invocation for the static initialization object will initialize the library at the start of execution. Conversely, the destructor invocation will perform any required cleanup before the end of execution. □

Index